Praise for *Sex Witch*

"At a time when sex and sexuality are under attack, we need writers like Sophie Saint Thomas and books like *Sex Witch* to remind us that pleasure and magic are our birthright. *Sex Witch* is funny, smart, and filled with more rituals, spells, and information on sex magic than you can shake a dildo at."

—Sarah Lyons, author of *Revolutionary Witchcraft: A Guide to Magical Activism*

"Sophie's *Sex Witch* is the perfect guide for anyone wanting to deepen their relationship with their inner ability to perform magick, and increase pleasure, power, and love— not just through the common tips we see posted online, but through rituals and spells that go a layer deeper and call forth our innermost delicious desires, our inner goddesses, and our hidden sources of power within."

—Alexandra Roxo, author of *F*ck Like a Goddess: Heal Yourself. Reclaim Your Voice. Stand in Your Power.*

"Sophie's words and instructions for sex magick in this book penetrate deeply and yet remain fun. I immediately felt excited to put into practice the spells laid out for me and the encouragement to find my unique identity as a Sex Witch."

—Vanessa Cuccia, author of *Crystal Healing and Sacred Pleasure*

T0026908

"There are witches and then there are sex witches—those of us who love to flirt with the edge, with the abyss, with what society would often consider 'indecent' or 'immoral.' But the truth is that witches have always lived in the margins. Yet there hasn't ever been a book written for the kink witches. In *Sex Witch,* Sophie Saint Thomas offers the missing link between witchcraft and the sex-positive movement, and an endless amount of magick and inspiration for those who want to embrace their sacred (and messy) sexuality. A must have for any witch; *Sex Witch* is the book we've been waiting for."

—Gabriela Herstik, author of *Bewitching the Elements: A Guide to Empowering Yourself through Earth, Air, Fire, Water, and Spirit* and *Inner Witch: A Modern Guide to the Ancient Craft*

"Sophie Saint Thomas has lovingly crafted the first kinky, queer, and deliciously slut-positive compendium of healing, hexing, and sexing spells for sex witches of all stripes. Whether you want to heal from a breakup, hex TERFs and homophobes, conjure clarity about your kinks, empower yourself before a sex party, consecrate your sex toys, create a cannabis-based flying ointment, strengthen a romantic relationship, or just get good and laid, *Sex Witch* offers the radical sex-positive tools for this magical work. Sophie's application of kink guidelines to witchcraft is especially compelling, as 'risk aware witchcraft' is a necessity for protecting yourself when delving into the subversive, highly stigmatized, and even forbidden realms of sex, drugs, pleasure, and pain. A shameless celebration of sexual freedom, *Sex Witch* encourages us to cultivate the potent, political powers we all possess within our hearts and minds and between our thighs."

—Kristen J. Sollée, author of *Witch Hunt, Cat Call,* and *Witches, Sluts, Feminists*

Sex
Witch

Sex Witch

Magickal Spells
for Love, Lust, and
Self-Protection

SOPHIE SAINT THOMAS

 WEISER BOOKS

This edition first published in 2021 by Weiser Books,
an imprint of
Red Wheel/Weiser, LLC
With offices at:
65 Parker Street, Suite 7
Newburyport, MA 01950
www.redwheelweiser.com

ISBN: 978-1-57863-720-1
Library of Congress Cataloging-in-Publication Data available
upon request.

Cover design by Kathryn Sky-Peck
Cover photograph © 2021 Ebru Yildiz
Interior by Kasandra Cook
Typeset in Sabon

Printed in Canada
MAR
10 9 8 7 6 5 4 3 2 1

To the famous astrologer Annabel Gat, my best friend, platonic life partner, and the original *Sex Witch*

Contents

Acknowledgments

Thank you to my agent and fellow Scorpio Eric Smith of P.S. Literary for being my biggest champion and Peter Turner of Weiser Books for turning *Sex Witch* into a reality. I would also like to thank Queenright Coven and LORE—my occult communities—and NSFW—my sex community. Thanks to my family for loving me for who I am. Thank you to my New York City chosen family: I love each and every one of you. You give me life. A very special shout-out to my orange tabby cat familiars, Mama Cat and Major Tom Cat. A very special sorry-not-sorry to any exes I hexed. Thank you to Chad, Melissa, John and Pat, Cameron, Teresa, Sam, Rosemary, and all my editors who let me write about spells all these years. But most importantly, this book is for all the Sex Witches all over the world. May this book help you understand just how powerful you are.

Introduction

I came with the penis candle inside of me. It was red. Like any responsible witch, I had put a condom on it. As I came, I visualized my dream partner. I summoned Lucifer for this spell. While such a sentence is the stuff that leads to frantic calls from family members accusing me of devil worship, I can explain. Lucifer, the angel who didn't want to hang with the church angels, just wanted to do his own thing. He's a symbol of individuality. As a sex journalist and witch, I need a partner who is chill with an unconventional lifestyle. One too many exes either judged or tried to change me. Then I headed out to a concert, and saw my spell in action, with a reminder that the universe has a sense of humor.

After my attempt to get backstage and bang Marilyn Manson was thwarted due to a giant gun stage prop falling on the Antichrist Superstar, I instead met an actor online who played the Devil in a witch cult classic film. He turned out to just be an actor trying to make ends meet. We never met up in real life, although the brief Skype love affair was a bit on the nose, considering the deity used in the spell. It was after this encounter that I finally met the man who matched my dream partner checklist: He accepted me. There was genuine love, chemistry, and great sex. He was self-supporting. We traveled the world together and began to make plans for our future. The relationship went up in flames.

A breakup delivers a massive blow to the ego and produces feelings of failure. However, not all romantic relationships are meant to last for your entire life. Some people come into our lives to teach us about ourselves and the world or to leave us with an experience. Through hard work—and excluding cases of abuse—we can come to see our former lovers as gifts rather than failures that render us unlovable.

In retrospect, when I look at both my candle sex magick spell and the resulting relationship, I forgot a few things. I focused on enticing immediate qualities in a partner and ignored many red flags that suggested from the start this was not a relationship with endgame potential. Spells are more than candles and incantations. To manifest what we want, we must integrate knowledge and reason. We can't just dance under a full moon. We must know which type of relationship is best for us and how to communicate with partners to maintain that relationship. In this book, you will find spells utilizing occult knowledge, such as how to conjure a partner using sex and candle magick—otherwise known as candle fucking. You will also find relationship advice built on my decade of experience as a sex and dating journalist to ensure you're staying true to your needs. Using scientifically backed information in your spellwork does not make you less of a witch; it means that your spells will work. Witches have always played the role of the wise one ready to step in when churches and governments fail folks. Sex ed mostly sucks, and reproductive and LGBTQIA+ rights are under attack. Our work as witches is to utilize both esoteric and scientific knowledge when mainstream institutions fail us.

Sex Witch combines occult knowledge with tried-and-true relationship advice to provide you with spells for each stage of relationships. Self-love, seduction, sex, love, protection, revenge, and healing are all covered. This book does not subscribe to the false distinction between so-called "black magick" and "white magick." While the only people we'll hex are rapists or homophobes, *Sex Witch* aims to both help you find a partner and satisfy your need for justice in cases of heartbreak through rituals to live your best life. (Remember, the best revenge is living well.) We'll break our toxic cycles. We'll fuck candles to summon the perfect partner. We'll embrace and unleash our kinks. We'll navigate relationships through rough patches. We'll get over former lovers. We'll balance karma when someone wrongs us. We'll forgive ourselves when we mess up.

This book also does not subscribe to heteronormative gender roles. *Sex Witch* is for all genders and orientations and includes spells specifically for gender identity and sexual orientation. All are welcome. Because let's be honest about something: Many of us are not always welcome. Pleasure is persecuted, and there is a war on sex that is far more tragic than the war on Christmas, let me tell you. Have you noticed that everything, from orgasms to weed—basically the most harmless drug on Earth—is actively policed? Have you ever hung out with Evangelicals? All they do is talk shit about people for their so-called sinful behavior, also known as being a human with a sex drive. And the Christian agenda doesn't end at awkward Christmas dinners. Those assholes push their script onto all of us through lobbying—and it works. Horrific transphobic bathroom bills pass. Reproductive rights are rolled back while rapists take the highest offices in the world. The time to come out as a Sex Witch is now. We need you at the front lines, squirting and hexing and covering your home in glitter and standing up for yourself—not only in relationships but in the world.

If you bought this book to reclaim pleasure and fight back, massive respect. You don't have to be in or want a long-term relationship to use this spellbook. The immense growth and fun to be had while single is often overlooked. *Sex Witch* aims to honor every phase of our romantic lives, and that includes the time in which the only person we aim to please is ourselves.

Once, after a breakup, I cast a spell during which I used fruit to absorb any lingering resentments that no longer served me to healthily date again. Following instructions from one of my mentors, I threw the fruits, charged with lingering hurts and fears, in front of the gates to a cemetery. Then I walked home without looking back. It was night. At a crossroads close to my home sat a black cat. I knew it was a sign that my spell had worked.

I find that life's more fun when you believe in magick. Regardless of your thoughts about deities, black cats, or incantations, there is undeniable power in ritual. Maybe having sex with a red candle summoned the spirit of Lucifer and led me to the aforementioned experiences and then, ultimately, to my current lovely partner. Maybe writing a list of traits I need in a partner led me to act upon them, and by the power of self-awareness, hard work, and human will, I ultimately found a healthy and compatible relationship. Maybe leaving fruits at cemetery gates magickally shed the pain that was keeping me from dating. Or, perhaps, I decided that it was time to move on, and the fruit spell served as a ritual to remind me to stop ruminating over the past. Maybe the black cat was just a stray and not a sign. I like to believe in both. If you have the will and desire to open your mind both to magick and the idea that you are worthy and deserving of sex and love, this book is for you. Now let's become Sex Witches and not look back.

1. Magick School

This is your Hogwarts acceptance letter. We have been following you for some time. You show magickal promise. Would you like to be a Sex Witch? Wonderful. We're glad to hear it. Look: All your powers are already inside you. A witch is simply someone aware of their power and not afraid to use it to get what they want. There is nothing wrong with wanting. It is natural human and animal behavior. You deserve to have a partner who loves you and has a hurricane tongue.

Before we move onto the spellbook portion of this book, which will help you summon such a partner, let's review some magickal basics. Why are Capricorns like that? What is a Satanic witch? And how can I work with my ancestors if they're all a bunch of abusive racists? Keep reading, witch. And refer back to this section as needed.

Types of Magick

There are as many ways to be a witch as there are witches. When I first got into witchcraft, I walked straight into my local occult bookstore and asked to see their books on Wicca. The rightfully judgmental clerk asked me, "Specifically on Wicca?" and I realized how little I knew about practicing witchcraft. There are distinct religions, or groups, from

Wicca to Aleister Crowley's Temple of Thelema. You do not need to belong to any of these. Most witches are solitaries and fluid in their practices. You can practice the plant-based medicine adored by Wiccans for lunch and have controversial Crowley sex magick for dinner. There are, however, a few forms of magick that this spellbook repeatedly talks about. Read on to know what the hex I'm talking about regarding color magick, chaos magick, sex magick, and more. Refer back to this section as needed. Remember that it's also okay for your practice to change like the seasons.

Sex Magick

Believe it or not, sex magick is not just spells to attract more sex. Sex magick is harnessing your orgasms for manifestation. Sexual energy is powerful. It's potent. It's so goddamn strong that you can use it for more than pleasure. You can use sex magick for sex, but you don't have to. You can use it for whatever the hell you want. What do you want? Perhaps a book deal, more money, or to marry your current partner? Work on your visualization skills: visualization is crucial to witchcraft. Sex magick can be practiced alone or with a partner, but masturbation is usually preferred. Why? Well, imagine someone humping you while you try to make a candle spell. Another person can be an annoying distraction. Plus, as it's hard to find good dick, witches often sleep with muggles. If you perform sex magick while making love to a muggle, do not let them know what you're up to. Their doubt could affect the spell! If you are dating a fellow witch, you can do sex magick together. And yes, you can use sex toys for sex magick. They don't call it a magick wand for nothing.

Chaos Magick

Chaos magick is precisely what it sounds like, chaotic—and it's bloody brilliant. While some magickal traditions focus on the ritual, chaos magick is all about achieving results by whatever means necessary. This means that you can get messy and mix magickal traditions without adhering to a strict order, and your intention is to manifest your desires. You are in charge. The philosophy grew in contrast to following a set of rules. I bet that you're already doing chaos magick!

Color Magick

Each color represents different aspects of the human experience. Consult the following list to know which color candle to use or flowers to bring into a spell and even deepen your understanding of tarot.

Green: Green is for money spells, prosperity, abundance, growth, and nature. It represents the earth and is also useful in fertility spells. Green is helpful for health spells. Use green to make money, protect yourself against STIs (in conjunction with actual medicine, of course), or have a baby.

Blue: Blue represents tranquility, peace, and calm. It's used for protection spells and also encourages communication. Turn to blue for a house blessing candle or to restore calm in a relationship after a fight.

Purple: Purple is the color of royal luxury. It can also enhance intuition and creative projects. Use it to add power to your poetry.

Pink: Pink is the color of love, self-love, friendship, and affection. Use it to enhance the enjoyment in a relationship in which the sex is great, but more tenderness is desired, or to boost confidence when you're feeling down.

Red: Red is the color of passion and love. Use it to make your sex life out of control or to enhance the excitement in a relationship.

Orange: Orange is the creative, weirdo, genius. Use orange to write a best seller or to call upon some Ziggy Stardust swagger.

Yellow: Yellow represents the sun and joy. Use yellow to bring more confidence and happiness into your life.

Black: Black is a controversial color. Some witches don't use black candles due to their association with black magick (more on that to come). A black candle is safe. Everyone needs to calm down. Use black for protection—and fine, hexes.

White: White represents purity and peace. It's also a stand-in color and works for every spell. Use white to purify your home after a lousy hookup.

Candle Magick

Throughout this book, we will work with a lot of candles. Candle magick is one of the most accessible and useful forms of spellcasting. Candles come in all shapes ranging from genitalia to cats to what's known as seven-day pullout candles. Using candles shaped like figures is pretty straightforward. Use a penis to make someone with a penis hard for you, and use a couple-shaped candle to bring you and your partner together. Seven-day candles come in a removable glass container, and

I highly recommend them. Here is an essential step-by-step guide to creating a candle spell using a pullout candle:

1. Select your candle based on color. Consult the color magick guide on pages 3 and 4.

2. You will need incense and oil. You can buy various potions and powders at your local occult store or online.

3. Spread out a newspaper so as to not ruin your floors.

4. Sage your candle and all your candle-carving equipment. Who knows what kind of nasty energy your candle picked up on its way to you!

5. Pour some honey into the base of the glass. This helps the candlestick adhere to the bottom of the glass and also honors Venus. Taste it before squirting it in as a taste test for the gods.

6. Feed the candle. Sprinkle herbs or flower petals that correspond with the spell at the bottom of the glass. For instance, dried rose petals are excellent for all love spells.

7. Keep a coaster or small plate nearby to cover the glass. Use a cocktail spoon to scoop up your incense. Depending on your spell, you can use incense for love, protection, money, etc. Stick the lit spoon in the base of the glass candleholder and hold it there to make it supersmoky. Remove the spoon and place a plate on top.

8. Carve your name, zodiac symbol, and a sigil into the candle. A sigil is a magickal symbol. You can find ready-made ones in books such as *The Enchanted Candle,* or you can make your own as instructed on page 69. If you're in a hurry, a simple dollar sign or heart works. You can buy specialty candle-carving tools online or use a bobby pin, knife, toothpick, or even a pen.

9. The gayer the candle, the better it works. Let's glitter bomb the thing. Choose a color to accent your spell, and sprinkle glitter down the middle of your newspaper.

10. Coat your candle in appropriate magickal oil to make it extramagickal and extrasticky.

11. Roll your candle back and forth in the newspaper to cover it in glitter.

12. Take the plate off the glass case and plunk your candle in there. Watch the smoke magickally billow out. Light the candle. Keep it burning at all times except when you aren't home. Even if a spell works, it won't be worth burning your house down over. As the candle burns away, your intention transmutes across the veil. Once the candle finishes burning, your spell is complete.

Ceremonial Magick

While there are many solitary witches and casual covens, some traditions, such as the Hermetic Order of the Golden Dawn, practice magick through elaborate ceremonies. Such societies have a select membership process and initiation, and what occurs is often top secret.

Sympathetic Magick

Sympathetic magick is an umbrella term for witchcraft based on imitation. For instance, working with the moon is sympathetic magick, as we use the waning phase when the moon appears to shrink for banishing work and the waxing phase when the moon seems to grow larger to draw desirable things.

Satanic Witchcraft

Some witches do work directly with the energy of Satan, or often to be more specific, Lucifer. Satanism (surprise) has a controversial history thanks to figures such as Anton Szandor LaVey, founder of the Church of Satan, who pushed the concept of following your animal passions into some seedy territories. Regardless of what you think of LaVey, he did help bring nontheistic Satanism mainstream. We still see nontheistic Satanism today with the (also controversial) Satanic Temple and its smaller offshoots or through the individual Satanists all over the world. Legend states that Lucifer, the fallen angel, was cast out of heaven for refusing to conform. Thus, as presented in Goethe's *Faust* and Milton's *Paradise Lost,* Lucifer represents the individual rebelling against the oppressive powers that be. He is an ally of all those cast out and persecuted by the church. Invoke Lucifer when you feel like a rebel ready to metaphorically burn down some churches. This use is, admittedly, more of a theistic invocation of Satanism than a nontheistic one. Satanism is not scary because of the devil. Satanism is scary because it states that you can be your own higher power. It says that, as demonstrated in the Magician card, you are capable of using your own will, cleverness, and even sexuality to get exactly what you want. In Satanic witchcraft, all you need to cast a spell is yourself.

Wicca

Wicca is a modern neo-pagan religion deeply rooted in nature. Wiccans work with both a female and male god: the Moon Goddess and the Horned God. Wiccans believe in the rule of three: "Three times what thou givest returns to thee," or what you give in your practice and spellwork does come back to you three times. Wicca is made up of many sects and traditions and is as diverse as the day is long.

Shades of Gray

Everything you know about black magick and white magick is wrong. The term *black magick* often refers to spells that harm others. However, this usage is misinformed and racist, as it's usually applied to spells from Voodoo and other African traditions. Likewise, the term *white magick,* which people use to describe magick for good, invokes imagery of the blonde Glenda from *The Wizard of Oz.* Some witches believe that love spells, or any spells that "bend someone's will," are immoral. There is no universal morality: it's a bullshit Christian concept unfit for witches. Life, and witchcraft, exists in shades of gray.

Sometimes you have to show some teeth. Sometimes you have to be a little problematic—but at a much higher vibration than the shitty books and films. Sometimes protection spells are required. You didn't ask for an abusive ex, but you can reclaim some power with a proper protection spell. And if someone doesn't want to get hexed, then maybe they shouldn't be a predator. We are only protecting you and going after those who use violence to bend the will of others. As it comes to matters in love, well, here is the truth: magick is real in that it's a tool to focus our powers of manifestation and intention. You can light all the red candles in the world, and if he's not into you, he's not into you. Be careful what you wish for—if you perform an obsession spell on some doofus you met on Tinder and he not only becomes obsessed with you but turns out to be insufferable, that's on you. The BDSM community uses the acronym RACK, which stands for risk-aware consensual kink and means everything from spanking to blood play, as long as all parties know the risks and enthusiastically consent to them, is fair game. That's between them. As you use this book and as your magickal practice develops, I encourage you to try RAW—or risk-aware witchcraft. You set the parameters for your mortality—wild, I know.

Casting a Circle

Witches cast circles to create a protective bubble to safely cast spells inside. We only let in demons whose names are on the guest list, thank you very much. Casting circles is kind of like putting on condoms: most witches don't use protection every time, even if they know they should. One easy way to cast a circle is to light sage and wave it around the area in which you are performing magick. You can also sprinkle salt around a circle. Many witches invoke the four elements when casting a circle.

The Grimoire

A grimoire, or book of shadows, is a witch's journal of spells. Using spellbooks created by others is a beautiful way to learn things and much like a cookbook. Following the recipe teaches you about the craft, ingredients, and how everything works. But as you develop your practice, you realize that so much of magick relies on intuition. You decide which deity to work with. You determine the candle color. The more you meditate and cast spells, the more heightened your intuition becomes. Treat your grimoire like a journal. It's inherently magickal because it's yours, but you can consecrate it using sage; leaving it out in the light of the full moon; spritzing it with holy, full moon, or Florida Water; or placing your favorite crystals on it for a day or two. Please keep a record of the spells you cast and their results. Gradually your grimoire will become an extremely personal repository of spells that helps you come into your own as a witch.

Invoking the Elements

Regardless of which form of magick you are developing, most witches cast a circle and invoke the elements of air, water, fire, and earth. This section explains how to invoke the elements and what each one represents. We'll also dive into how the elements coordinate with the tarot and astrology and are integral to witchcraft.

 ## Air

Tarot: Swords

Signs: Gemini, Libra, Aquarius

Direction: East

Invocation: I call upon the guardians of the East, the element of air, of logic and intellect. Give me a sword of strength and swiftness of action to wield it as I please.

 ## Water

Tarot: Cups

Signs: Cancer, Scorpio, Pisces

Direction: West

Invocation: I call upon the guardians of the South, the element of water, of intuition and emotion. Give me a cup of knowledge and compassion, so I may become powerful in ways that mortal men fear.

Fire

Tarot: Wands

Signs: Aries, Leo, Sagittarius

Direction: South

Invocation: I call upon the guardians of the South, the element of fire, of passion and creativity. Give me a fiery wand so I may blaze my own trail and burn with eternal strength that no hater may blow out.

Earth

Tarot: Pentacles

Signs: Capricorn, Taurus, Virgo

Direction: North

Invocation: I call upon the guardians of the North, the element of earth, of all that is material and strong. Give me a stable foundation to stand on and the freedom to enjoy the fruits and riches of life without shame.

Making an Altar

An altar is your magickal working space. Simply pick a table somewhere quiet and decorate it with personal and magickal objects. This can include crystals, candles, images of deities and ancestors you call upon, and perhaps objects to represent the four elements. A ritual dagger works for air, a goblet for water, matches or a special lighter for fire (and to light candles), and flowers or coins for earth. There is no prescriptive method for creating an altar as we are all so beautifully different, like precious little snowflakes. It's time to reclaim the term *snowflake,* anyway. All witches have different levels of love for cleaning, but at least once in a while, clean off your altar to keep it looking fresh.

In addition to a central altar, some witches create an altar specifically for honoring love. It usually has lots of reds and pinks—the color of love—and sacred objects that remind you of love. These can be keepsakes passed on from ancestors, dried rose petals, fresh flowers, rose quartz and garnet, and if you're kinky, your lover's underwear—or something of that sort.

Meditate and spellcast in front of your altar, and remember to make space to place tarot decks, candle spells, and other witchy tools.

Cannabis and Other Herbs

Whether it's ingesting the plant to reach an altered state of mind or using dried herbs to feed a candle spell, working with plant medicine is a big part of most witchcraft practices. Reference this section, which lists and defines the uses of common herbs for witchcraft from relaxing lavender to the stimulating damiana, as you begin your spellwork.

Aloe: Aloe is amazing on the skin and healing, especially for burns and sunburns. Aloe is a protective plant.

Anise: Anise treats stomach troubles and helps with insomnia. It helps keep nightmares away.

Apple: Apple, as presented in the tale of Adam and Eve, represents freedom, delightful temptation, and reclaiming one's sexuality free of shame. Would thou like to live deliciously? Use apple seeds in your spells.

Arnica: Arnica relieves pain from sprains and bruises. Magickally, it is most potent during the summer solstice. It's useful for protection work.

Basil: Basil is antibacterial and treats common colds, in addition to making delicious pesto sauce. In many traditions, basil is known to enhance and attract love. It is a common ingredient in love spells.

Bay leaves: Bay leaves represent infinite good luck. Use one for a boost of extra oomph in a spell.

Cannabis: Cannabis can relieve pain and enhance intuition and psychic connection. Long before our government regulated it—for reasons that had nothing to do with the plant being dangerous; it's not—cannabis was a tool of spiritual insight.

Cayenne: Use the spicy red powder to drive away enemies. Don't get it twisted and use it to "spice things up" romantically—it will only lead to bickering.

Chamomile: Chamomile is a much-needed herb of relaxation. Sip it in a tea to unwind after a long hard day or during emotionally taxing spellwork. Add it to spells when you need to calm down a situation.

Cinnamon: Cinnamon is precisely the right kind of heat to add to a love spell. It also helps speed up spells, so add some when you're in a rush.

Cloves: Cloves are associated with the element of fire and are used to stop unwanted gossip and burn away enemies. Cloves also attract luck and friendship.

Comfrey: Comfrey brings safety and protection to your home and also keeps you secure during travels.

Damiana: Damiana is a natural aphrodisiac and works wonders in sex spells to increases attraction and desire.

Echinacea: Witches work so hard that we get sick too! Take echinacea to keep your health strong and fight away unwanted physical viral attacks or psychic vampires.

Garlic: Garlic fights sickness. Eat roasted garlic or boil a garlic tea if you have the common cold or flu. Hang garlic in your house to protect against vampires and negative energies.

Ginger: Ginger adds the right amount of romance and lustful spice to a love spell.

Hawthorn: Hawthorn is like your herbal best friend. If you're feeling down in the dumps or recovering from gaslighting, use hawthorn to remove negative influences and take back stability.

Lavender: Lavender is a calming herb. Smoke some, burn some, or drink lavender tea for tranquility.

Lemon balm: Lemon balm is a natural antianxiety herb. Enjoy it as a tea or tincture to let go of stress after a long day of dealing with fuckbois.

Mugwort: Smoke mugwort before bed to encourage lucid dreaming. Mugwort can also encourage psychic visions.

Nutmeg: Nutmeg brings you luck! Carry some around when you need a good day. It's especially useful in money-drawing spells.

Rose: Roses are the go-to for all love spells. To dry roses, hang them upside down on a hanger. Red roses invoke passion and romance, but all colors represent love. Consult the color magick list on pages 3 and 4 to learn which rose is best for your magickal needs.

Rosemary: Rosemary can be bundled, lit, and used to purify spaces just like sage. It promotes love, both in friendship and romance. It's associated with the goddess Aphrodite.

Sage: Sage is used to purify and cleanse spaces. Recently, witches have become more aware of the importance of ethically sourcing sage and avoiding overharvesting, so to the best of your abilities, be in the know about where your sage comes from. Sage cleanses a space of all energies, offering a blank slate.

Valerian: Valerian is a relaxing sleep aid. Use it after an awful day fighting in the war of love to relax and care for yourself.

Wormwood: Wormwood has a fabulous reputation because it's an ingredient in absinthe. Burn wormwood to cultivate stronger psychic abilities.

Potions, Period Blood, and Other Liquids

From Come to Me Oil to La Flamme, an obsession oil, learn up on various potions, oils, and even bodily substances commonly used in spells for sex and love. You can buy most of the oils and potions listed online or at your local occult store. As for those that come out of your body, well, that's why witches have so many mason jars.

Attraction Oil: Want to attract some more money? A new mate? Smother your spell in this.

Banishing Oil: Ugh, is a pesky ex blowing you up? Perhaps your new boo's ex won't leave you alone? Banish them.

Come to Me Oil: Look, dude, I know you're into me; you know you're into me. Let's stop playing games and just come to me already.

Fast Luck Oil: If this dry spell goes another day, I may die from horniness and I'm broke. Give me fast luck.

Fiery Wall of Protection: Fiery Wall of Protection brings out the big guns. Is a toxic ex or someone even more dangerous fucking up your shit? Opt for Fiery Wall of Protection.

High John the Conqueror Oil: Smash those obstacles in your way with High John the Conqueror.

La Flamme: La Flamme is an obsession oil, and it works, so use wisely.

Love Oil: For straightforward, beautiful, Hallmark love, look no further than a classic love oil.

Menstrual blood: Use your period blood to power up a spell or to bind a lover to you.

Money-Drawing Oil: Get rich or die trying, witch.

Pan Oil: Pan is an earth god of fertility, so nature-focused witches can use this spell to enhance their sex life or attract abundance.

Protection Oil: Use protection oil to keep haters from ruining your relationship.

Saint Martha: Saint Martha the Dominator hates bullies and loves the underdog, the sex worker, the queer, the beautiful spirit that society shits on. Let her dominate your enemies and reunite lovers.

Sappho Oil: Sappho Oil is for lesbians. Are all gay people inherently magick? Let's go with yes.

Scarlette's Seduction: Use this lusty oil to seduce a lover for insanely hot sex.

Semen: For people with penises, semen is a way to up the ante on any spell, for love or money.

Success Oil: Success oil brings success and triumph to any endeavor.

Urine: Urine dominates. Just like a dominatrix pisses into the mouth of a client, or a domme onto a sub, use urine in your spells to exert your power over another.

Vaginal fluids: Vaginal fluids work much like menstrual blood. Try squirting on a candle. They are good for sex spells (duh).

Venus Oil: Invoke Venus, the goddess of love and abundance, for love and money spells.

Moon Phases

Witches love the moon. All the rumors are true. Have you ever looked up at the moon and felt peace? The moon is a comforting and powerful tool because her cycles mirror our own. Or better stated, our cycles reflect the moon. Sure, this is why many witches who menstruate identify with the moon. However, you certainly don't need to have a uterus to invoke her power. The moon's cycles—from the dark fresh start of the new moon to the bright manifestation of her fullest form—mirror the natural ups and downs of life. These phases are also incredibly useful in sympathetic magick, which is based on correspondence. The waning moon phase, when the moon appears to get smaller, is excellent for banishing work. Spells of attraction or money drawing, which require growth, are appropriate for the waxing moon. Read on for a detailed description of how to use each phase of the moon. Refer back to this section throughout your practice.

New Moon: The dark new moon is a time of new beginnings. Only the stars puncture the sky, and a new cycle awaits. During the new moon cast spells for new projects, fresh starts in relationships, and to bless all beginnings.

Waxing Moon: During the waxing phase, we watch the moon grow, creeping closer to its fullest state. The waxing moon is most excellent for spells that desire growth. Use the waxing phase to bring in more money and to grow intimacy within a relationship.

Full Moon: The full moon represents peak manifestation. Use the powerful full moon to send spells bursting forth. It's an excellent time for sex magick. Cast a spell to land a professional deal or to inject a relationship with divine protection.

Waning Moon: During the waning phase, the moon appears to get smaller as it returns to the fresh start of a new moon. Spells of protection, banishing work, and jinx removal are especially potent during this time. Cast a spell to banish pesky exes or busybodies interfering in your relationship during this time.

Rose Quartz Dildos and Other Magick Rocks

Everyone—even Gwyneth Paltrow—knows about crystals now. Yes, expensive rose quartz yoni eggs exist. But don't let that ruin your love of rocks. Let that amplify your love of rocks! If you want and can afford it, why not shove some crystals inside of you to remove lingering ex residue. Anyway, look. No, there is no substantial scientific evidence on the efficacy of crystals. All witchcraft requires an ability to relax and have some fun. Crystals have been a part of alternative spirituality and non-Western medicine practices forever. Healers believe that they interact with our energy field. Are you a crystal witch? There's only one way to find out. While today, crystals often find themselves trapped in the middle between witchcraft and capitalism, there is nothing wrong with buying a crystal if you want one. Many New Age stores sell them for cheap. Even though I'm more of the type of witch who goes straight for the period blood, meditating with rose quartz is healing and fills me with self-love. I sleep with black tourmaline on my bed frame for protection. Why does black tourmaline make me feel safer from the evil rapists I worry will come to break into my apartment? Read on and reference this section as needed.

Agate: Agate helps you let love in and accept yourself for the beautiful angel that you are.

Amber: Amber is not a crystal, but fossilized tree resin. It's a healing stone that pulls out negative thoughts and is helpful when you're feeling down.

Amethyst: Amethyst is a powerful stone to enhance spiritual awareness and intuition. Historically, it's used to promote sobriety and ward off overconsumption, so wear one before a martini date to avoid acting sloppy. It also encourages motivation.

Aventurine: Aventurine, as the name suggests, encourages bravery, prosperity, and creativity.

Bloodstone: Bloodstone is a balancing and spiritual stone that expunges negativity and lifts you up spiritually.

Calcite: Calcite removes negative energy and amplifies your rock star qualities.

Carnelian: Carnelian removes your fear of death. Meditate with carnelian in a cemetery or with the Death card in the tarot.

Citrine: Citrine is a stone of the sun and abundance. Wear it on a ring to attract wealth.

Garnet: Garnet is a red stone that enhances love, sex, and passion.

Jade: Jade brings tranquility to the home and human on which it is placed. It helps aid in meditation to fight negative thinking and can stimulate intuitive dreams.

Jasper: Jasper enhances sexual prowess, ow ow! It also acts as a comfort stone during times of stress and can work as a motivation stone, encouraging you to achieve your dreams.

Jet: Jet is fossilized wood. Like other black stones, it acts as a protective stone and soaks up nasty negative energy.

Kunzite: Kunzite helps clear our emotional baggage and cynicism away, so we may flourish in our current and future relationships.

Labradorite: If you're feeling insecure and fearful from past hurt, labradorite can also help clear that unwanted garbage and raise your spiritual vibration to Bob Marley levels.

Magnesite: Magnesite, which resembles a brain, helps you achieve rational thought during the hellish roller coaster that is dating.

Malachite: Malachite is more toxic than the Britney Spears song, so it should only be handled in its polished form. If you dare use it, malachite is a transformational stone that can aid in breakups.

Moonstone: Moonstone is connected to the moon, and therefore, a stone of divine feminine intuition. Use it for profound emotional healing.

Obsidian: Obsidian is hard lava. It repels negativity and exposes flaws—both in others and yourself. It's a molten truth serum. It's excellent for shadow work but not for the faint of heart.

Onyx: Onyx gives its witch strength and protection by healing past wounds. However, onyx exists in a memory world that can trap you in nostalgia if you're not careful. Opt for onyx when you're ready to face and work through your past.

Opal: Opal helps you reach your full potential, witch.

Peridot: If you're experiencing unwarranted feelings of guilt preventing you from moving on, meditate with purifying peridot.

Quartz (clear): Clear quartz is like a white candle, it can pretty much do anything. Perhaps its strongest property is amplification. Clear quartz can amplify your hard work, self-esteem, and dreams.

Quartz (rose): Rose quartz is a very famous love stone! If you remember your color magick, you may guess that because it's pink, it's wonderful for self-love, unconditional love, and connecting with your heart chakra when times feel tough.

Selenite: Use selenite to connect with your higher consciousness, especially when you have no idea what to do in a situation and need divine clarity.

Sulphur: The stone form of sulphur helps you tap into your jealous, petty, needy, contrarian little bitch sides. Use it for shadow work to integrate your so-called negative traits for positive benefit.

Sunstone: Like rays of sunlight, sunstone lifts you up when you're feeling down and dark. Meditate with this stone when you're prying yourself away from toxic relationships.

Thulite: Thulite is a rare but potent stone that helps you use your brain instead of just your boner. It's magnificent for applying logic to love and lust.

Topaz: Topaz is an excellent breakup stone as it soothes hurt, recharges, and curates calm in times of change.

Tourmaline: Tourmaline, most often black tourmaline, is a protective stone that scares away self-loathing, jealous exes, and other ghoulies. Try a black tourmaline wand and use it to brush away negativity from yourself and home.

Turquoise: Self-sabotaging? Turquoise is the stone for you. It helps us work through our own insecurities to become the most vibrant version of ourselves.

Zoisite: Are others trying to control you? A rarer stone, zoisite helps you rise above the influences around you and live true to yourself.

The Tarot

The tarot is the best place a baby witch can begin learning and a sure thing for a seasoned witch to come home to. The seventy-eight cards continue to be a source of knowledge, wisdom, and controversy. It's believed that the first deck originated in Italy sometime in the fifteenth century. Back then, was it just an edgy deck of playing cards that depicted a female pope, or has the tarot always contained occult themes? In the centuries that followed, the deck spread and developed, with occultists such as Aleister Crowley creating their own. Today, from Crowley's Thoth deck to the classic Rider-Waite to modern decks such as the Black Power deck, the Steampunk Tarot, Cat People tarot, and even a David Bowie tarot, there is something for everyone.

Tarot is split up into the Major Arcana and the Minor Arcana. The Major Arcana tend to represent people or significant life shifts, while the Minor Arcana show smaller snapshots of our current situation. Today, the cards are primarily used as a divination tool. While there's nothing wrong with pulling cards to ask about a boy—we all do it—they are more complicated and sacred than a Magic 8-Ball. Together, the Major Arcana works as a story of the arc of a well-lived life. Often, the cards read us more than we read them. It's common to pull a card only to feel very called out!

I find using the cards as a meditation tool or mirror more helpful than divination because the choice of how to act remains my own. If we view the tarot as a beautiful work of art depicting the human experience, even the "worst" cards, such as the Tower, become sources of insight rather than evoking fear or being a stamp of a doomed relationship—although some readings do feel that way.

There are many spreads and ways to read the tarot. For a more detailed read on the cards, I suggest *Seventy Eight Degrees of Wisdom* by Rachel Pollack. But you don't have to follow a spread. Often I intuitively start pulling cards, place them next to one another, and meditate on what picture they paint. If you're new to tarot or just looking to become more grounded in your practice, I suggest a morning tarot meditation. Sit in silence each morning for ten minutes or so meditating. When you're ready, start shuffling a deck. Simply ask what you need today. Pull a card. At the end of the day, meditate again and reflect on how that card appeared throughout your day. Sometimes tarot cards and what they represent are very handy in spellcasting. We'll use them throughout this book, so refer back to this section as needed.

MAJOR ARCANA

The Fool: The Fool, the first card of the Major Arcana, represents beginnings and taking risks. The Fool wants you to take a brave leap and start your own business or leave that fuckboy to revel in the adventurous unknown.

The Magician: The Magician is pure willpower and manifestation. The Magician wants you to realize your potential and, using your practical and magickal tools, make your dreams happen already.

The High Priestess: The High Priestess is divine feminine intuition. Tapping into her power will illuminate all areas of your life. However, the High Priestess exists across the veil—it's up to you to make use of her wisdom in the real world.

The Empress: The Empress is a sex goddess. She is abundant, glorious motherly love and affection. She is blooming flowers and passion. She is multiple orgasms during a new relationship or childbirth.

The Emperor: The Emperor is a stern daddy. He keeps business in check and provides stability, but his commitment to rules and logic feels ruthless at times.

The Hierophant: The Hierophant is a card of collectivism and following the rules. It signifies churches, establishments, and other ruling bodies. The Hierophant may appear when we start a new job or have a lover with a frustratingly religious family.

The Lovers: The Lovers don't leave much for interpretation. They are a couple happily in love and lust. When this card appears in a new relationship, revel in it. If you're single and it keeps appearing, especially in the past position, the Lovers may suggest nostalgia for an ex.

The Chariot: The Chariot is a sign of success. It indicates mastering a situation through the force of will. Your determination paid off. Enjoy the feeling of accomplishment.

Strength: While the Chariot looks outward, Strength represents taming the inner self and emotions. Are you feeling overwhelmed, scared, and like you're riding a roller coaster of emotions? Invoke Strength to take control of inner pain and turmoil.

The Hermit: We all need a break from lovers and friends to stay in and be with ourselves. The Hermit indicates withdrawing temporarily from the outside world to restore inner peace. Sometimes it may mean that someone in your social circle is not to be trusted.

Wheel of Fortune: The Wheel of Fortune spins and spins and turns our world upside down, whether we want it to or not.

This card appears right before or during monumental cosmic life shifts.

Justice: Justice is about honesty. The Justice card indicates that you deserve whatever is going on. No more rosy glasses—it's time to face facts. Don't like what your life is serving you? If you practice radical honesty, you can make moves to change things.

The Hanged Man: The Hanged Man wants you to surrender and let go. This card isn't about execution, but more Dale Cooper dangling upside down as a form of yoga to help solve the murder of Laura Palmer.

Death: Chill, please. Death is not scary—okay, maybe a little bit—nor does it indicate physical death. Death is the card of rebirth and renewal. You may pull it during a time of transformation after a breakup or quitting a job. Treat yourself to a makeover!

Temperance: Temperance isn't so much about self-control, but the advanced skill of applying logic to passion. You may pull Temperance when you are having life-destroying beautiful sex with someone but are unsure of how to turn it into something more "serious." Honestly, quite often, Temperance wants you to do nothing and wait.

The Devil: The Devil is a beautifully kinky, materialistic, vain card. Older interpretations view the Devil as an addiction or a situation that you are shackled to and need to get out of. More modern understandings of Satan as an adversary interpret this card as consensual BDSM or an independent spirit living life on their own terms and challenging authority.

The Tower: The Tower means your world is going to crumble. It's a scary card—but an indication that things are going to change, and when the debris clears, you will be stronger and happier than ever before. The Tower indicates breakups, dramatic shifts in worldviews, and sudden cosmic change.

The Star: The Star brings calm after a storm. This card indicates that healing is taking place after a rough patch. Hope and serenity are on the horizon.

The Moon: When the Moon appears, your unconscious is trying to tell you something. The Moon is what's behind the High Priestess's glorious robes. If you pull this card, spend time meditating, and pay attention to your dreams to see what's up.

The Sun: The Sun is physical, abundant, joy. This card indicates wonder, happiness, and a lust for life. Enjoy it.

Judgment: Judgment asks you to look inward. Your outer surroundings are the same, but you are growing. The change may have already happened. It's on you to craft an outward reality that reflects the inner you.

The World: The World is a card of holy completion—not *holy* in the sense of the church, but of divine honesty and honoring your true self. Your inner worlds match your outer worlds.

MINOR ARCANA—WANDS

The suit of wands is associated with the element fire. Wands are passionate, creative, horny, and ambitious.

King of Wands: The King of Wands is a natural leader, and he knows it. He's powerful, and his confidence and ambition are boner-inducing. He can be a bit intolerant and insufferable at times, but you always forgive him because he has good dick.

Queen of Wands: The Queen of Wands is a sexy bitch. She loves life and is secure in herself and her success. Unlike the King, she can be both ambitious and empathetic.

Knight of Wands: The Knight is eager and ambitious with a lot to learn. He has immense potential and will succeed in this world, but mainly on his ego and privilege.

Page of Wands: The Page of Wands symbolizes that fiery energy that occurs at the start of projects and relationships. This card appears when we're ready to move onward.

10 of Wands: The 10 of Wands indicates that you have overextended yourself. Take some time to recharge to avoid burnout.

9 of Wands: The 9 of Wands points to someone who has endured a lot in their life, through trauma, oppression, or simply because they are one of those souls meant to experience and feel all that life has to offer. You can use those experiences to advance your life but make time to tend to emotional wounds through self-care and therapy.

8 of Wands: The 8 of Wands is like, "We're done here." This card may signify the end of a job so that you may move on to bigger and better things with more money or the end of stressing out about the state of a relationship because you're both ready to commit.

7 of Wands: The 7 of Wands is a card of quarreling—except everyone gets off on it. This card could mean a dick-measuring contest at the office, a race to finish a deadline that fills you with adrenaline, or a relationship in which you enjoy power dynamics in bed.

6 of Wands: The 6 of Wands represents victory through the power of will and optimism. Your goal—be it romantic or professional—is not complete; however, you wear a crown. Make sure you pair hard work with that cocky attitude to avoid counting your chickens before they hatch.

5 of Wands: The 5 of Wands indicates friendly and consensual competition—perhaps through group sex. In a darker light, this quarreling can be petty and a waste of everyone's time, such as to win the affection of an idiot who doesn't even know how to eat pussy.

4 of Wands: The 4 of Wands indicates that you're in a shitty situation, perhaps one that is holding you back. The good news is that through inner strength and optimism, you can escape the burning building before it turns into a Tower-like fire.

3 of Wands: The 3 of Wands represents learning to be at peace with your past. You feel whole and complete and are ready to admire and enjoy the current life you've created.

2 of Wands: The 2 of Wands is one of those people who fight and fight to achieve success, and then once they do, they are bored. They miss the chaos and have no idea how to relax.

Ace of Wands: The Ace of Wands is a burst of primal, creative, and sexual energy. Drawing this card indicates a good omen for new relationships or creative and professional projects.

MINOR ARCANA—CUPS

The suit of cups represents the element of water. They are intuition, emotion, and relationships. They usually pertain to matters of the heart.

King of Cups: The King of Cups is very wealthy and successful, but at the expense of his dreams. He's the guy who wanted to be a painter but went to law school because his mom told him to.

Queen of Cups: The Queen of Cups is also quite successful, but she achieved her dream through the use of imagination. Her emotional intelligence feeds not only her professional achievements but also allows her many loving romantic and platonic relationships in her life, which are a source of strength.

Knight of Cups: The Knight of Cups is very busy exploring his inner world, so do not take it personally if he cannot commit. He has a lot to learn.

Page of Cups: The Page of Cups is too young to be hurt by the sensitivity of emotion. He is still learning and allowed to fantasize. This card represents a student and often appears at the start of a relationship or project, which requires us to have a beginner's mind.

10 of Cups: The 10 of Cups shows pure joy and happiness. But what's truly special about this card is that the people receiving such wonder appreciate it.

9 of Cups: You work hard. You have accomplishments under your belt. The 9 of Cups says that it's time to feast and celebrate.

8 of Cups: It's time to move on. There is nothing left for you. Yes, the 8 of Cups is a sad card, but acceptance makes it easier.

7 of Cups: The 7 of Cups presents a situation that appears too good to be true—because it is. The cups appear filled with love, wealth, and opportunity, but upon a closer glance, it's basically a scam.

6 of Cups: The sweet 6 of Cups reminds us to accept love and open our hearts to a childlike state. However, it can also indicate nostalgia that is holding you back from fully experiencing the present.

5 of Cups: The 5 of Cups shows loss. However, there is an acceptance of the loss, which is the saving grace of this card. Use strength to learn and move forward. It's time for the next chapter.

4 of Cups: The 4 of Cups presents the reader incredible opportunities; however, the reader cannot see them. They are bored and spoiled by life and currently incapable of appreciating even more opportunities coming their way.

3 of Cups: You won! Maybe at love, maybe at work, but it's time to celebrate with friends. Have a threesome!

2 of Cups: The 2 of Cups is a smaller version of the lovers. It represents happiness and sexual pleasure within a relationship, usually at its start.

Ace of Cups: The luscious Ace of Cups represents fertility, creative success, beauty, abundance, delightful vanity, and happiness. Look hot and enjoy!

MINOR ARCANA–SWORDS

The suit of swords corresponds with the element air. They represent the intellect and the mind. Warning: swords are vicious blades. This suit bites!

King of Swords: The King of Swords is an authority figure—and rather judgmental at that. He can be cold and harsh, but he does care about justice and can raise his sword to cut through the bullshit, particularly around social issues.

Queen of Swords: The Queen of Swords has been through hell and back. While giving in to defeat and sorrow is tempting, the sword of intellect helps her rise above her pain and rule with dignity.

Knight of Swords: The Knight of Swords is brave, but thoughtlessly so. Having lived a privileged life, he does not yet understand consequences.

Page of Swords: The Page of Swords uses his mental strength to detach himself from worry. While this is a useful skill, if we become too detached—common in air signs—we run the risk of losing partners or friends because it seems like we don't give a fuck.

10 of Swords: Oof. Ten swords straight to the back: this isn't just a card of defeat; this is a card that says it's O-V-E-R. The good news? Occultists say that the phrase "It's always darkest before the dawn" originated from this card. It sucks to get stabbed ten times, but you're on the up.

9 of Swords: The 9 of Swords hurts. The 9 of Swords is waking up in the middle of the night, still drunk, and remembering that you cheated on the love of your life. Accept it. Deal with it. Be a grown-up.

8 of Swords: The 8 of Swords acts as a prison. It is the person who is so caught up with petty gossip and criticizing details that they miss the beautiful painting of life right in front of them.

7 of Swords: The 7 of Swords represents a wonderful scam. There is action, but often impulsive and ill-prepared.

6 of Swords: The 6 of Swords opens a gate that takes you away from a painful situation—one you've grown so accustomed to the pain has become normal. Will you pass through the gate or stay put?

5 of Swords: You fought, and as the 5 of Swords indicates, you lost. This is a card of defeat.

4 of Swords: The 4 of Swords shows withdrawal. The hardship has passed, and now you want to hide. A period of withdrawal can be healing, but beware of it leading to isolation.

3 of Swords: The 3 of Swords represents heartache, no doubt about it. The only way out is through it.

2 of Swords: Things are okay. For real—you can let your guard down. But the 2 of Swords does not. This card remains blindfolded with two swords across their chest. Like Nick Cave once said, let love in.

Ace of Swords: The Ace of Swords is influential. It can bring us to enlightenment or destroy enemies. How you use it is up to you.

MINOR ARCANA—PENTACLES

The pentacles, sometimes called coins, correspond with the earth element. The pentacles represent material matters such as money, health, and manifestation. They also relate to our pride, happiness, and self-esteem.

King of Pentacles: The King of Pentacles has fucking made it. He worked hard to get the high life, and this dude means to enjoy it. Mediocrity is his enemy.

Queen of Pentacles: The Queen of Pentacles is a badass bitch who understands that sexuality, success, and love are all-natural and intertwined. She has no shame in the enjoyment of earthly pleasures and is beautiful for it.

Knight of Pentacles: The Knight of Pentacles gets shit done, but by dutifully following responsibility, he forgets the joy in work.

Page of Pentacles: The Page of Pentacles, in contrast to the Knight, is a student in awe of the wonders of the Earth and the joy of satisfying labor.

10 of Pentacles: The 10 of Pentacles reminds us that there is magick in everyday life all around us, and we're assholes for not seeing it.

9 of Pentacles: The 9 of Pentacles represents a rich, successful single lady who needs no man.

8 of Pentacles: The 8 of Pentacles teaches that you can't just become an overnight success, you have to work—except in cases of extreme privilege—and appreciate your work if you ever want to make it.

7 of Pentacles: The 7 of Pentacles is a moment of reflection. The subject feels immense satisfaction from their work and takes the time to notice. There is enough of a security blanket built up that the worker can step back without fear of failure.

6 of Pentacles: The 6 of Pentacles is kinky. It denotes success and monetary gain, but usually from a person in a position of power. It can also indicate a consensual power-play relationship.

5 of Pentacles: The 5 of Pentacles represents a rejection of authority, traditionally the church, and the costs that can, unfortunately, come with living an independent life.

4 of Pentacles: The 4 of Pentacles shows someone selfish. But you know what? They deserve to be selfish.

3 of Pentacles: The 3 of Pentacles means that you are working hard and about to get some money and recognition.

2 of Pentacles: The 2 of Pentacles suggests a time of change, perhaps switching careers. It's also a symbol of enjoyment, which encourages us to go with the flow and allow transformation to take place.

Ace of Pentacles: The Ace of Pentacles means money, honey. Life is good. Don't overthink it: revel in the pleasure.

What Planet Are You From?

Scorpio is intense. Perhaps that is because it's ruled by Mars, the planet of war, and Pluto, the planet of death. Sound right? In astrology, each sign is ruled by one or, in some cases, two planets. For instance, Leo is governed by the sun, which is why they think the universe rotates around them. We all have each of the planets in our birth chart. Understanding what each planet rules can help you decipher that area of yours. For instance, if your Mercury, the planet of communication, is in Sagittarius, you are likely an attractive—and insufferable—party guest. While our sun sign has a planetary ruler, which carries significant sway in our astrological makeup, to understand how all the planets affect you, go online or download an app such as TimePassages to learn your chart. What's your birth time, baby?

The Sun

Rules: Leo

Spill the tea: The sun is king. We'd be dead without the sun, and the sun knows it. The bright golden rays of the sun are often associated with the divine masculine. Sun energy is big, bold, bright, warm, and friendly. The sun is dripping with jewels and the best and most ostentatiously dressed man in the room.

Time to change signs: One month

The Moon

Rules: Cancer

Spill the tea: The moon is divine feminine energy. She is intuitive—psychic, actually. She rules our emotional, creative side. She can be moody, but she apologizes for nothing. The moon knows that there is nothing wrong with showing some emotion. Judging someone for telling the truth and having feelings is for tight-ass Christians.

Time to change signs: Two to three days

Mercury ☿

Rules: Gemini, Virgo

Spill the tea: Mercury, in ancient mythology, is the messenger of the gods. He rules communication, intelligence, and transportation. That's why when Mercury goes into his infamous retrograde, these areas of our life go haywire. Emails get stuck in the draft folder; we play whack-a-mole with exes, and travel delays are not uncommon. Mercury is an absolute diva. He rules the voice. It's interesting that Freddie Mercury, a Virgo, picked the planet as his surname. Those with strong Mercury in their chart are often quite captivating.

Time to change signs: Three to four weeks

Venus ♀

Rules: Taurus, Libra

Spill the tea: Venus is that bitch. She is the goddess of love, pleasure, and abundance. She's flirtatious and absolutely beautiful. If you look at Venus in your chart, you can tell how you like to flirt, make love, date, dress and style yourself, and spend money. Venus also rules harmony, so she loathes petty arguments. She'd much rather be lounging with a postorgasmic glow as lovers feed her chocolate and grapes.

Time to change signs: Four to five weeks

Mars

Rules: Aries, Scorpio

Spill the tea: Warrior Mars will mess up your life with a rock-hard erection. Named after the god of war, Mars rules ambition, aggression, and hot sex. Mars is the divine masculine to the divine feminine of Venus. The planet of action, Mars also rules bravery. On a bad day, Mars is angry and confrontational and leaps before he looks. On a good day, Mars is pure willpower. Harness that energy and Mars will give you the courage to go after whatever you want.

Time to change signs: Six to seven weeks

Jupiter

Rules: Sagittarius

Spill the tea: Jupiter is like, so popular. It's why no one can stand a Sagittarius. For the size queens, Jupiter is the largest planet in our solar system, more than 300 times bigger than Earth. In mythology, Jupiter is the god of gods, who, despite that ridiculous title, was somehow honorable and wise. Optimistic Jupiter rules opportunity, joy, and success. Jupiter moves fast—the god of gods (g.o.g.) will drop the opportunity of a lifetime into your lap—but take it away just as quickly if you don't pounce.

Time to change signs: 12 to 13 months

Saturn

Rules: Capricorn

Spill the tea: Saturn is a very strict dom. It's no wonder that the "Celestial Taskmaker" responsible for us learning tough life lessons, rules Capricorn, the business daddy of the zodiac. Saturn rules work, discipline, responsibility, law, and ambition. On a bad day, Saturn is a stern conservative disciplinarian. On a good day, Saturn is the inner drive that helps you get shit done and make some money. Unlike Jupiter, Saturn does not work quickly. Saturn demands a slow and steady climb to the top, which is why so many Capricorns experience success later in life.

Time to change signs: Two to three years

Uranus

Rules: Aquarius

Spill the tea: Uranus is the eccentric revolutionary of the zodiac. In mythology, Uranus is your asshole. Just kidding, Uranus is the planet of fortune and rules what's modern and reason. This includes science and all that is original, rebellious, and unorthodox. It's no wonder that Aquarians are so strange. Uranus is also the planet of community, and those with heavy Uranus influences tend to have a profound effect on society at large. In the planet's most hopeful sense, it is Oprah; in its most problematic sense, it is Ronald Reagan. Uranus is the first of the "generational planets," meaning that it has a generational influence.

Time to change signs: Seven years

Neptune

Rules: Pisces

Spill the tea: Dreamy Neptune got its name from the Roman god of the sea, who is probably a total hunk. It is my personal opinion that Neptune is a bit of a stoner. Neptune is the planet of glamour, mystery, illusion, and artistry. Because it's the planet of tortured artists, Neptune also rules hospitals, addiction, and even prisons. Neptune is everything otherworldly and ethereal. Neptune is your dream coming true. But on a bad day, Neptune is a pizza burnt in the oven because you were so high you forgot to take it out.

Time to change signs: 10 to 12 years

Pluto

Rules: Scorpio

Spill the tea: Pluto is the ruler of the goddamn underworld. He's more goth than Bauhaus! Like the Death card in tarot (Scorpio's card), Pluto isn't as intense as his reputation would have you believe. Just kidding—he is intense, but in a cool way. Pluto is all about death, rebirth, and transformation. Pluto can put you through hell during significant life transformations, but you can trust that you're going to come out on the other side a far better version of yourself. Pluto loves an extreme makeover.

Time to change signs: 12–15 years

What's Your Sign?

What's your sign? It's the question of the century. It's fun to know your sign. Sometimes, I think that's the most important part of all of this. We're all going to die one day, let's have some fun with sex and witchcraft before we rot (sorry, I'm a Scorpio). Your "sign" refers to which one the sun was in when you were born. If you were born in Aquarius season, you're an Aquarius (and seriously, text your bae back already). Understanding your sign is the gateway drug of witchy shit, and it can help you understand your motives, as well as how you interact with others. Many spells also ask about your sign, so it's good to know for casting love spells. Remember that while your sun sign is a rad gateway drug, it's only the beginning. Do—or have an astrologer do—your entire chart to learn all the nooks and crannies of that absurd personality of yours.

Aries

Dates: March 20–April 20

Symbol: The ram

Element: Fire

Planetary ruler: Mars

Modality: Cardinal

Tarot card: The Emperor

Hot: No one is more fun than an Aries. These generous rams will show up with gifts without an occasion, make you laugh until you cry with good stories and gossip, and then show you their latest kink.

Not: An Aries will have a temper tantrum because their boss sounded condescending in an email and then dump you, complete with a character annihilation, as part of their unrelated rage.

 ## Taurus

Dates: April 20–May 21

Symbol: The bull

Element: Earth

Planetary ruler: Venus

Modality: Fixed

Tarot card: The Hierophant

Hot: Is it even sex if there's not a table filled with delicacies, fine wine, and strong weed in arm's reach?

Not: Yes, they are that lazy.

 ## Gemini

Dates: May 21–June 21

Symbol: The twins

Element: Air

Planetary ruler: Mercury

Modality: Mutable

Tarot card: The Lovers

Hot: Damn, Gemini is talented, hot, well-dressed, and charismatic. Can we get matching tattoos yet?

Not: There's nothing wrong with catching syphilis, but that doesn't mean I want it.

Cancer

Dates: June 21–July 22

Symbol: The crab

Element: Water

Planetary ruler: The moon

Modality: Cardinal

Tarot card: The Chariot

Hot: A loving Cancer will cook you the best home-cooked meal you ever had, make love to you on rose petals, and then read poetry in a different language.

Not: A Cancer will ask to marry you right after they come. Four hours later, their mother calls and reminds them how much they disapprove of you, so they end things.

Leo

Dates: July 22–August 23

Symbol: The lion

Element: Fire

Planetary ruler: The sun

Modality: Fixed

Tarot card: Strength

Hot: Charismatic Leo and their perfect hair will fill you with a lust for life you haven't felt since childhood.

Not: Damn, did you just achieve a major career milestone? Leo would say congrats, but they're too busy sulking because someone else has the spotlight.

Virgo

Dates: August 23–September 23

Symbol: The virgin

Element: Earth

Planetary ruler: Mercury

Modality: Mutable

Tarot card: The Hermit

Hot: A Virgo's apartment isn't just expensive and pristine, dear, each item of furniture doubles as kink equipment—but no squirting in the kitchen.

Not: Did you know that there's cat hair on your clothes? And that you have pretty bad mood swings? And that you're in the wrong kind of therapy? Now you do.

Libra

Dates: September 23–October 23

Symbol: The scales

Element: Air

Planetary ruler: Venus

Modality: Cardinal

Tarot card: Justice

Hot: On the first date with charming Libra, you will see a shooting star, and then they go down on you.

Not: They would have gone down on you for longer, but they have a second date to get to.

Scorpio ♏

Dates: October 23–November 22

Symbol: The scorpion

Element: Water

Planetary ruler: Mars and Pluto

Modality: Fixed

Tarot card: Death

Hot: A Scorpio is your ride or die with a love poem written in blood who will fuck you to the edge of your life while promising eternal love. You sell your soul to Satan and buy an engagement ring.

Not: Did that Scorpio fuck your brains out last night? Kinkiest sex of your life? Yeah, they just want to haunt you with memories of life-changing orgasms once you break up as part of their preemptive plan to ruin you.

Sagittarius

Dates: November 22–December 21

Symbol: The archer

Element: Fire

Planetary ruler: Jupiter

Modality: Mutable

Tarot card: Temperance

Hot: Bend over, witch, we're going on an adventure. I'm paying. Yes, multiple orgasms will be involved.

Not: Did I mention the second half of the trip is for business? You should probably go home. There is my secret family and all.

Capricorn

Dates: December 21–January 20

Symbol: The sea goat

Element: Earth

Planetary ruler: Saturn

Modality: Cardinal

Tarot card: The Devil

Hot: The ultimate business daddy, devilish Capricorn, will make you wet with leather ties and big dick energy. You never have to pay for dinner again.

Not: I hope you like conservative kids who get off on money and misery.

Aquarius

Dates: January 20–February 19

Symbol: The water bearer

Element: Air

Planetary ruler: Saturn and Uranus

Modality: Fixed

Tarot card: The Star

Hot: This independent water bearer will show you experiences you never thought possible and inspire you to be a better person.

Not: Aquarius somehow manages to be the cruelest person you know while simultaneously saving the planet.

Pisces

Dates: February 19–March 20

Symbol: The fish

Element: Water

Planetary ruler: Jupiter and Neptune

Modality: Mutable

Tarot card: The Moon

Hot: This dreamy babe will get you high, take you to a concert, and the next thing you know, you're fucking under the stars in the ocean.

Not: A flaky Pisces will take one year and multiple emotional breakdowns before offering you any romantic commitment.

Down with Deities

"Wait, gods? I became a witch to avoid the church." Me too, love, me too. But you know what, maybe Jesus is just alright with you like the Doobie Brothers said, or maybe you think he's a submissive little bitch. There are tons of deities out there other than him. The Bible doesn't want you to know this. From the Hindu dark mother goddess Kali to the Roman goddess of love Venus, there are tons of deities out there just waiting for pretty little pagans like us. You never have to work with a god, but here are some nice ones to know. And remember, if working with deities outside of your culture of origin, always practice appreciation rather than appropriation!

Aphrodite: Aphrodite is the Greek goddess of love and beauty. She embraces all sexuality and can aid you in any sex spell.

Baba Yaga: Baba Yaga appears as a terrifying crone in Russian lore. She is a wild woman who doesn't care what others think and will be by your side to fight the powers that be.

Bast: Bast is the goddess of protection and cats. Cat-lady witches can invoke the terrifying mystery and power of the feline through Bast.

Brigid: Brigid is an Irish goddess of fertility and healing. She has major Empress vibes. Ask Brigid to help you mend a broken heart.

Dionysus: Dionysus is the Greek god of wine. He loves sex, orgies, chocolate, grapes, cannabis, orgasms, parties, glamour, basically anything and everything that is fun in life. Invoke him because you deserve it.

Eros: Eros is the Greek god of love, passion, and physical desire. He's great for any love spell, but especially useful in bringing back the passion to a relationship.

Freya: Freya is the Norse goddess of love, sex, death, beauty, and fertility. When shit gets real, painful, and messy, ask her to help you find the love in it all.

Ganesha: Ganesha is the Hindu remover of obstacles. A lovely elephant, ask Ganesha for help stomping away bumps in the road.

Hades: Hades, also called Pluto, is the ruler of the underworld. He's useful in times of change and transformation or to remove fear.

Hecate: Hecate is the Greek goddess of witchcraft, necromancy, ghosts, and the moon. She is dark divine feminine intuition.

Kali: Kali is a Hindi dark mother goddess. She is the slayer of demons and isn't afraid of sex or violence. Kali is deeply protective and loyal. Her devotees often feel as if she picked them, not the other way around. Ask her permission before working with her.

Pan: Pan is the god of nature, and all that is wild and free. Call upon Pan to embrace your animal side or encourage growth in all matters.

Persephone: Persephone is the Greek goddess of rebirth and the queen of the underworld. She is Zeus's daughter and Hades's husband, so royal AF.

Saint Martha: Saint Martha, the dominator, is the patron saint of service workers. She's a slayer of dragons and bullies. Ask her for help when someone mean-spirited, hateful, or judgmental is getting in the way of your joy. Saint Martha knows that love trumps hate.

Venus: Venus is the Roman god of love, sex, fertility, and abundance. Work with Venus to attract all things luscious and loving.

Zeus: Zeus is the Greek god of sky and thunder. He has a million different god babies. Invoke him when you need to put people in their place and be the boss.

Ancestors: Hot or Not?

Ancestral magick is powerful and a preferred method of choice for many witches. Why? Well, let's say that someone is talking shit about you. Let's say your boyfriend's mom thinks you are a witch sent straight from hell—and she doesn't mean that in a good way. You could work with Saint Martha, or even Kali if you want to go all out, but your grandma (RIP) would really want to kick this bitch's ass. So like a prayer (cue Madonna), you ask your grandma to help you take care of her.

When we work with ancestors or deceased relatives, there is an instant personal connection that is extremely powerful. You can also avoid any risk of cultural appropriation if you stick with blood. However, many witches have pretty solid reasons for working with deities or traditions outside of their own. We're fucking witches. Many of us are queer. A traditional lifestyle doesn't often lead one to open a book titled *Sex Witch*. We don't want to work with our families because they may be the ones rejecting or talking shit about us. Or perhaps we come from an abusive home, an alcoholic home, or a strict Christian home that rejected us a long time ago. And that's not mentioning our ancestors. Those assholes can be next-level. I have a relative who was a sheriff and an executioner! Do I want to bring that energy into my spellwork? Not on a good day, that's for sure. However, working with these "negative energy" ancestors could also dispel whatever hold they have on us. For some witches, ancestors are a source of pride, knowledge, and protection. If that's not you—don't sweat it. There are other options.

However, if you do want to work with your ancestors, but don't know any who aren't utter pricks, consider researching your lineage. You may find some secret badass great great grandmother who rebelled against the family or an ancient aunt who was obviously a witch (no one knows that much about poisons). Or you may discover you have much more Irish blood than you thought and begin connecting with a deity such as Brigid and work with your ancestry through her.

David Bowie, Cats, and Other Forms of Energy

You can also practice witchcraft without using ancestors or a deity. On my altar, I have prayer candles for my two adopted fathers—David Bowie and Freddie Mercury—and I'm always invoking them. And your celebrity higher power doesn't even have to be dead! If you're a freelancer doing a spell to collect debts, I cannot recommend playing Rihanna's "Bitch Better Have My Money" enough. For everyone with a feline familiar—you know how cats stomp all over a tarot spread? Those little fucks know exactly what's going on. Ask your cat for some help. It's about time that they put those paws to work and chip in for rent in one way or another.

Of course, you can always act like a Satanic witch and be your own god(dess). You don't even need to label it with the *S* word. Just be a bad bitch and know that you've got this.

Essential Activism

Witchcraft is inherently political. Sorry, "apolitical" witches, your time is up. Let's start by talking about the enemy of the witch. Who would completely lose their shit if their son dated a witch? Who pushes restrictions on reproductive rights, LGBTQIA+ rights, and acts like separation of church and state is nonexistent while blowing their load for every other thing our founding fathers wrote? Christians. Look, there are Christian witches, and there's nothing wrong with being from a Christian family. But it is the Abrahamic religions that are using their gospel to persecute anyone who dares to be different. Witches are different. Witches are aware of their power and aim to use it, and this is what makes us so terrifying.

A witch must be aware of their surroundings. And that means paying attention to what's happening politically. There is no specific dogma or party affiliation a witch must take, but universally speaking, witches feel strongly about a few things. We care about minorities and equal rights. Many of us have experienced discrimination firsthand. We care about the Earth. We care about protecting and respecting indigenous people. We care about sexual and reproductive freedom. Think of every witch as part of a worldwide coven. We all don't have to hang out (introverts breathe a sigh of relief). We look out for one another. And to do this, activism is strongly encouraged. Show up. Educate yourself and vote. March. Be ready to bite back. Sometimes you need to show your teeth. On a local level, this means involving yourself in local politics, or hexing a rapist, or standing up for a minority getting bullied on the subway. On a global level, this means shopping ethically (whenever possible, I know that budgeting is a bitch), and speaking out against tyranny and hate in our national politics. If you want to be a witch, you have to be a badass. Can you handle it?

2. Sex Ed

Sexual Orientations

No, pansexual does not refer to the god Pan, and no, bisexuality does not reinforce the gender binary. Sexual orientation refers to the gender(s) you are attracted to. Don't see one that you like on this list? Don't worry! You can use whatever words that you're most comfortable with, and it's okay if you change which ones those are over time. Sexuality is a spectrum (hence the rainbow, duh).

Androsexual/androphilic: Androsexuality is the romantic, sexual, and aesthetic attraction to masculinity.

Aromantic: An aromantic person does not experience romantic interest in others.

Asexual: Asexuality, often abbreviated as *ace,* is a spectrum of people who experience little to no sexual desire.

Bicurious: Bicurious describes straight-leaning folks who are curious about sex with other genders.

Bisexual: Bisexuals are attracted to all genders. Even when bisexuals partner with a particular gender, that doesn't turn them gay or straight. They are still bisexual.

Demiromantic: Demiromantics need to form a strong emotional connection with someone before they can fall for them romantically.

Demisexual: Demisexuals need to form a secure emotional connection with someone before they are interested in them sexually.

Dyke: Dyke is traditionally a slur for queer women, especially masc queer women. However, the word is fun AF, so some are reclaiming it. However, if you're straight, double-check the situation before you start throwing the term around.

Gay: Gay describes someone who has an enduring physical and romantic attraction to the same gender. Gays are inherently magickal, so make sure that you don't fuck with them. Note: Some gays are okay with the term *homosexual,* while others consider it a slur, so ask before you use it—and understand that it makes you sound outdated.

Gynesexual/gynephilic: Gynesexuality is the romantic, sexual, and aesthetic attraction to femininity.

Lesbian: Lesbians are female-identifying goddesses who have an enduring romantic and physical attraction to other female-identifying goddesses.

LGBTQIA+: LGBTQIA+ is an acronym for lesbian, gay, bisexual, trans, queer (or questioning), intersex, and asexual.

Pansexual: No, being pansexual has nothing to do with the god Pan. Pansexuals are attracted to people regardless of gender.

Queer: Queer is an umbrella term to describe all LGBTQIA+ folks under the rainbow. It used to be a slur, but we reclaimed that shit. As we better understand that sexuality is a spectrum, older terms may feel too limiting. Queer also fosters a sense of community.

Skoliosexual: Skoliosexual is a new and supercool term to describe people who are attracted to trans, nonbinary, and genderqueer folks.

Straight (heterosexual): Last but not least (come on, you guys get to go first in everything else in this world) are the straights. Heterosexual folks are enduringly physically, romantically, and sexually attracted to the opposite gender.

Gender Identities

Gender also exists on a spectrum, and many people are currently considering their gender identity for the first time in their lives. It's the gender revolution—and the side of the rebels will win. Know your terminology. This section lists and defines various gender identities, such as transgender, nonbinary, and cisgender. Remember that gender identity is different than sexual orientation.

Agender: Someone who is agender describes themselves as genderless. They may feel gender-neutral or like they don't have a gender.

Androgynous: Androgynous, as opposed to gender identities, refers to appearance. Androgynous people present in a manner that is indistinguishable between male and female or fluctuates and fucks with gender roles.

Bigender: Bigender is those who feel two distinct genders. They may feel both at the same time or fluctuate. The genders could be male and female or female and nonbinary, etc.

Cisgender: Cisgender folks are those whose gender identity matches what they were assigned at birth.

Gender expression: Gender expression is how someone outwardly expresses their gender, usually through dress, voice, haircut, knuckle tattoos, social media profiles, ya know.

Genderfluid: Someone who has a nonfixed gender identity, which may fluctuate. Genderfluid folks may feel male one day, mostly nonbinary the next, and another combination of a different sort the next.

Genderqueer: Genderqueer is an umbrella term for those whose gender falls outside of traditional norms. Their gender may contain one or more genders or fluctuate between genders.

Intersex: An intersex person is someone with a natural variation on physical genitalia or chromosomes.

Mx.: (Pronounced "Miks") is a gender-neutral title.

Nonbinary: A nonbinary person's gender is not restricted to "male" and "female"; it is beyond the binary.

TERF: TERF is an acronym for trans-exclusionary radical feminist. It refers to "feminists" who are transphobic, exclude trans women from feminist and women's spaces, and do not include or actively disclude trans women in their version of feminism.

They/them: They/them are gender-neutral pronouns. Remember, never assume anyone's pronouns, you can always ask!

Transgender: Transgender is an umbrella term for folks whose gender is different than the sex they were assigned at birth and all the societal expectations that come with it.

Two-spirit: Two-spirit is an umbrella term from Native Americans, which refers to folks who have qualities of both genders.

Consent

Enthusiastic consent is crucial. What is enthusiastic consent? It's not the absence of a "no" but a surefire "yes." It doesn't need to sound like a fucking cheerleader, but it should be certain that not only are all parties agreeing to sex but that they're completely down with it. Who wants any other type of sex anyway?

Consensual sex is not any of these scenarios: pushing through a "no," continuing even when it's obvious one party is not having it, taking off a condom without asking, or switching orifices without asking. Additionally, don't just break out a spanking, choking, knife play, or any other kink without prior agreement.

Consensual sex is sexy, ongoing communication that makes it evident that everyone is here for what's happening. "So I have to ask permission before I even move my hand?" asks the straight guy bent on playing devil's advocate. (The devil hates devil's advocates, by the way.) Look, if you're in a long-term trusting partnership, you will develop ongoing or perhaps even prearranged "blanket" consent. Blanket consent is when you and your partner agree that during sex, certain things are cool and, unless someone invokes the safeword, open to improvisation. For instance, a couple into rough sex may arrange blanket consent regarding what that roughness entails ahead of time, so when they're in the moment, they can enjoy the scenery.

Another issue some raise with consent is the sexiness factor. "Asking permission? That's not hot! I want to be in the moment!" Such a mindset lacks serious creativity. It's so easy to make consent sexy. You can even turn it into dirty talk. "Fuck, baby, I want to put my finger in your ass." *Swoon.*

Such a statement allows the person whose ass is in discussion to say yes or no. As previously mentioned, if you have an ongoing sexual relationship with someone, you'll find a groove that works for all of you. And you can always invoke the safeword. A safeword should be something nonsexual and unique, like "pineapple." Some have a universal safeword, and others select one for each relationship. To come up with a safeword for your relationship, play a game of free association. I say "pineapple," you reply with "piña colada," I respond with "sailboat," and next thing you know, you're safeword is "sea urchin." It's good to have spiky animals on your side.

Kink Glossary

Sex is so much more than an orgasm or a sword going in a chalice. That's like the bare minimum these days. Kink is an umbrella term for basically anything outside of straight (boring) vanilla sex. (A fetish, on the other hand, technically refers to an attraction to an inanimate object, such as a high heel, a foot, or a couch.) Some people are kinkier than others. Kink, such as an epic erotic humiliation session, may be a core part of your sex life. For others, it's not always sexual. They might just want to beat the shit out of something. As long as you practice enthusiastic consent, there's nothing you can really fuck up. If it turns you on, enjoy it. Don't make me give you the Scorpio death speech again. Embracing your kinks is part of becoming a witch in the War on Sex.

Aftercare: Aftercare is just a fancy word for checking in and taking care of one another after the sex or kink scene is over. If you just did something like impact play, this could mean applying ice to your lover's bruise. If you tried something new with the potential to be an intense scene, like rape role play, it could mean checking in with one another to make sure you're both happy. If you're not, you can talk about how to make it better the next time. Quite often, aftercare is simply cuddling and pillow talk.

Age play: Age play is a role play in which one or all partners pretend to be an age different than their own. For instance, in daddy dom/baby girl role play, often the baby girl will pretend to be like, in high school, whereas the daddy dom is like, stepdad age. It ain't wrong if it's role play between two consenting adults.

BDSM: BDSM is an umbrella term for activity related to bondage, discipline, dominance and submission, and sadomasochism.

Bondage: Bondage is restraining or tying your partner up. You can use handcuffs, a belt, hemp rope, tape, Christmas lights—truly whatever your pervy little heart desires.

CBT: CBT indeed stands for cognitive behavior therapy, a form of talk therapy in which the client learns coping skills and emotional regulation. However, it also stands for cock and ball torture. In cock and ball torture, the dominant partner uses their hands, chastity devices, cock rings, their heels, and many other exciting tools to literally torture a submissive's cock and balls. This CBT is also a form of therapy.

Cuckolding: Unfortunately, the alt-right has adopted the word *cuck,* stealing it away from the respectable cuckolds of the world. Traditionally, a cuckold is a husband who enjoys watching another man, the bull, fuck his wife. He is often in the corner, crying and not allowed to participate. If his wife (the "hot wife" in this scenario) is feeling generous, she may let him jerk off. The female version of a cuck is a cuckquean.

D/S: D/S means dominance and submission, the consensual erotic power exchange between a dominant—often abbreviated *domme* if they are female-identifying and *dom* if they are male-identifying—and a submissive—or *sub*.

Dominant: A dominant is someone who enjoys taking on the dominant role in kink.

Edge play: Edge play doesn't refer to the edge of a blade, but the edge of what is considered socially acceptable. But don't let that deter you from trying edge play; it truly is rather fabulous. The definition of edge play will vary on who you ask—and how strong of a stomach they have—but includes blood play, getting choked out, or being pooped on.

Electrostimulation: Electrostimulation is the use of electricity for erotic purposes. For instance, you could use the Violet Wand, which is an electric magick wand that can make your nipples—and other areas—buzz-buzz with delight.

Erotic humiliation: Erotic humiliation is the art of absolutely humiliating the sub to the brink of orgasm—or tears—by calling them names, spitting on them, or doing whatever delightful degradation all parties prearranged.

Exhibitionism: An exhibitionist is someone who gets off on others watching them. Excellent ideas for an exhibitionist to try include going to a sex party or fucking on a hotel balcony.

Fisting: Who needs a dick when you have a fist? Fisting is the act of inserting an entire fist into an orifice, such as the vagina, anus, and even mouth. One should work up slowly to fisting by starting with one finger, then two, and then inserting the entire fist. Don't forget to use lube. Wearing a nitrile or latex glove (I suggest black) can make fisting easier and even pervier (why yes, doctor, I do need to be stretched out).

Foot fetishism: A foot fetish is a fetish for feet. Foot fetishists may enjoy foot worship, giving foot massages, smelling feet, getting a footjob, being stomped on, and so much more.

Golden showers: A golden shower is a lovely warm fountain of piss cascading over you. It is a form of piss play (obviously) and can be used in humiliation play or just for fun.

Impact play: Impact play refers to any impact on the body, such as spanking, slapping, flogging, whipping, or walloping a booty using a spatula.

Knife play: Yes, knife play refers to using a knife during kink scenes or sex. Yes, it is dangerous. Knife play is a form of edge play, or kink that's considered "on the edge" of what's sane and consensual. Yes, knife play is awesome. Kink partners or happily married couples may use a knife to draw blood—avoiding arteries—or hold it against their partner's throat during sex.

Limits: If anyone read about knife play and was like, "No, thank you, not for me," then you have discovered a limit! Limits are kinky acts that you do not want to do. They are your no-nos. It's good to know your limits so you can share them with partners. Often people will have their hard limits or acts such as poop play, which they will not do. You can also have soft limits, which are activities that you're curious about but not ready to engage in at this time.

Orgasm control: Orgasms control, sometimes used interchangeably with orgasm denial, is a practice in which the submissive will relinquish control of their orgasm over to their dominant. The dominant controls when and how they come. This can refer to edging, in which the dominant brings the sub to the brink or edge of orgasm and then stops. Others may have their sub wear a chastity device, and others may tie their sub up and hold a Hitachi magick wand against their clit until they come.

Pain slut: A pain slut is just some dope bitch who is a slut for pain. She may like spanking, flogging, slapping, biting, pinching, or many other grown-up activities. Talk to your pain slut to find out.

Piss play: Piss play is exactly what it sounds like, baby! Piss play includes golden showers, drinking piss, splashing in piss, or truly whatever your heart and bladder desire.

RACK: RACK stands for "risk-aware consensual kink." The kink community considers RACK to be the most modern kink guidelines. The idea is that what is considered "sane" is drastically different from person to person. One guy's needle play is the other guy's "call 911." RACK asks that every consenting party is okay with the risks associated with each kink.

Role play: Role-playing is pretty self-explanatory; it's when you take on a role, often a fantasy such as doctor, maid, or Satan. Costumes are encouraged but not mandatory.

Scene: A scene is a period in which the kinky play goes down.

Shibari: Shibari is the Japanese art of rope bondage.

Spectrophilia: Spectrophilia is an attraction to ghosts—spooky!

SSC: SSC is the old-school kink safety guidelines, and they stand for "safe, sane, and consensual."

Submissive: A submissive is a person who enjoys surrendering control, or submitting, during sex.

Switch: A switch is someone who enjoys both the dominant and submissive roles and can literally switch back and forth between them. Get you a witch who can do both.

Vanilla: Vanilla refers to boring—I mean socially acceptable—usually heteronormative intercourse. Vanilla sex is sticking a penis into a vagina without bothering to use lube. It's okay if you are vanilla; there are other ways to experience life fully, such as skydiving or martial arts.

Voyeurism: A voyeur is someone who gets off on watching. Don't watch others change, strip, or fuck without consent, though. Go to a sex party where voyeurism is accepted.

Zentai: Zentai is a skintight, full-body suit usually made of spandex and nylon. It covers the entire face. Some people like how wearing one feels, some people like how others look in them—why overanalyze kinks? If it turns you on, enjoy it.

Relationship Format Glossary

You never have to cheat ever again. You can have more than one partner, and everyone is on board. Of course, that doesn't mean that it's easy, but it does mean that you have options. Likewise, if you never want to deal with a "poly" bro who equates communication with Burning Man stories, you never have to do that either. Or you can just have threesomes or never date again in your life. In addition to gender and orientation, today's society is finally rethinking the way we format love. For many witches who have created a chosen family, the idea of creating your couture relationship is already like, "duh." Refresh, or if you're still exploring relationship formats, learn by checking out the following list.

CPOS: CPOS stands for "cheating piece of shit." Bow down to Dan Savage for coining the word. There is ethical nonmonogamy and unethical nonmonogamy, commonly known as cheating.

If you have a history of being a CPOS, perhaps you should ask yourself if monogamy is for you. You can remove a lot of guilt, shame, and hurt by switching to an open relationship in which everyone consents to the nonmonogamy. However, some people seem to get off on the sneaking and lying that cheating entails and are unsuited for ethical nonmonogamy. Can you integrate sneaking around into your open relationship? Weirder things happen.

Don't ask, don't tell: There is no one right way to do open relationships. Some people like to know what their partner is up to or even meet and become friends with their partner's partners (metamours). Others prefer a don't ask, don't tell policy. They consent to an ethically nonmonogamous setup but don't care to hear the dirty details.

Ethical nonmonogamy: Ethical nonmonogamy, often abbreviated to ENM, is an umbrella term for a consensually open relationship.

Hierarchical poly: In hierarchical poly, there is a primary partner. On the outside, a couple may even pass as monogamous. But they also have secondary partners, who they may date as a couple or separately.

Monogamish: Another phrase coined by sex witch Dan Savage, monogamish refers to a couple who is mostly monogamous, but allows room for human error and desire. For instance, if one partner is going to travel alone for a month and wants permission to take on a foreign lover, they can talk about that. Or, if someone gets drunk and makes out with a friend at a party, it's not the end of the world.

Monogamous: In a monogamous relationship, two people commit to only loving and fucking each other for the duration of their relationship.

Polyamorous: Polyamory translates to "many loves." Polyamorous people both love and fuck multiple partners.

Relationship anarchy: Relationship anarchy is a form of ENM that holds all relationships of equal value regardless of who is fucking or even married—the word *anarchy* is in there for a reason. A relationship anarchist may have a spouse, a platonic nesting partner, and a lover, and holds them all the same and equal value.

Sexually open: In sexually open relationships, a couple is down with sleeping with others, but sets boundaries to prevent emotional interference.

Solo poly: In solo poly, there is no hierarchy or primary partner. A person views all of their partners on an equal playing field.

Swingers: Swingers are couples who play (have sex) with other couples. They may swap for the night; they may all have sex; they may go to swingers' parties and resorts. However, from the outside, they often look like normies.

3. Magick for Self-love

Self-love sounds corny. I'm just going to say it. But it's popular for a reason: it's powerful. One is far more likely to attract a healthy partner when they are confident and aware of their self-worth. Confidence is the sexiest thing about a person. It's just big dick energy. So let's get you some of that. This section should be revisited regardless of your outside relationship status to ensure your relationship with yourself is the best it can be. Just like you shouldn't forget your friends, don't ever forget about yourself. In addition to finding self-confidence, these self-love spells address painful common modern-day issues that lead to self-doubt, such as gender identity and social media stalking.

Sigil Making for Self-Confidence

You will need: Newspaper, candle-carving supplies, sage, a pink candle, a notebook, a pen, Venus or love incense, small plate or coaster, honey, a love oil (optional), glitter (optional)

The best time to cast the spell: The waxing moon

> 66 *Sigil making is creating magickal desires. This spell first teaches you how to make personal symbols or sigils. This is a basic useful skill that can be employed for many spells. This one in particular combines sigil making, candle magick, and color magick by carving a pink candle (the color for self-love) in a spell for self-confidence.*

Sex Witch says

*Confidence is the most potent ingredient in sex appeal.
BDE (big dick energy) is just confidence.*

The Spell:

1. Prepare your working area. Candle wax is tricky to clean up, so cover the floor with newspaper. Set out your supplies.

2. Light the sage and cleanse your supplies, paying extra attention to the candle, as well as yourself. Make sure to get the bottoms of your feet.

3. Close your eyes and meditate. What do you wish to cultivate within yourself? Perhaps you need a reminder that you're worthy of love or that anyone would be lucky to have you. Confidence is extremely hot.

4. Open your eyes. Write down everything you felt. When you're done, boil your intention letter down to one sentence, such as, "This pussy is magick."

5. Go through the letters of your sentence one by one and transform them into a symbol. Cross out each letter once used. For instance, I'd start with the letter *t* and draw a *t* figure, crossing out every other *t*. Then I'd do the same for *h, i,* etc., until all the letters are used up and my sigil is complete. The sigil contains the power of your intention.

6. Pick up your pink candle. The best candles for magickal workings are seven-day pullout candles, which are available at your local occult store or the online botanicas listed in the resource section. However, any candle wide enough to carve your sigil works. Pink represents self-love, although a white candle will do if you don't have pink on hand.

7. Keep your mind focused on your intention. Repeat your sentence over out loud during the spellcasting.

8. Light your incense. If you're using a pullout candle, remove the candle from the glass holder. Add a dollop of honey on the bottom as an offering to the gods and to make the candle stick. Fill the glass with incense. Place a small plate, coaster, or other object on top of the glass to contain the smoke. If you're using a regular candle, simply bathe it in the incense as if using sage.

9. Take out your candle-carving tools. They can be purchased online, or you can use a toothpick or small knife. Carve your sigil into the candle. Do so intentionally, but don't fret if it's not perfect. Your will is the most powerful part of the spell.

10. On the reverse side of the candle, carve your name (or initials) and the symbol of your zodiac sign.

11. Dress the candle in an oil if you have it. For extra oomph, roll the candle in glitter, a color representative of your desires.

12. Light the candle. When it's finished burning, your spell is complete.

No TERFS Allowed: Embrace Gender Identity

You will need: Yourself

The best time to cast the spell: Anytime

> " *All genders can be witches despite the frequent portrayal of witches as cis women. Regardless of the pronouns we use, we all contain both masculine and feminine. I always identified as a cis woman, until once while topping with a strap-on I realized that I'm both a femme queen and a bit of a bro. Different people can use this guided meditation to explore your own gender fluidity in different environments.*

Sex
Witch
says

The Spell:

1. Sit somewhere conducive to a meditative state. Close your eyes and begin deep inhales and exhales.

2. Your gender is in your mind, not between your legs. Some witches have a fixed gender identity. Others ebb and flow between genders. Everyone contains both masculine and feminine. Our gender presentation is just (glamorous) drag. Envision your body as a canvas that you get to paint.

3. Begin a body scan meditation. You are your own god and creator. What do your feet look like? Beginning at your toes and slowly moving up your legs, to your hips, chest, and finally head, visualize your body exactly as you feel inside. Are you an androgynous Bowie-esque star? Perhaps a butch lady-killer? You can be whatever you want to be.

4. When you're ready, open your eyes. Use costume, clothes, and makeup to create the gender presentation that feels best for you. However, once again, that's just drag. The only thing you need to explore and express your gender is yourself.

5. Your gender and gender presentation can change as often as you want. Return to this meditation as desired.

Tap into the Divine Feminine

You will need: A tarot deck, goblet or wineglass, red wine or another red beverage

The best time to cast the spell: At night with a view of the moon

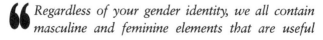 *Regardless of your gender identity, we all contain masculine and feminine elements that are useful*

in understanding ourselves and performing spellwork. Sometimes the intuitive and emotional energy of the divine feminine is what we need. While tarot decks contain many cards, such as the High Priestess and Empress, containing feminine-presenting figures, we use the Moon card for this ritual, as it's a universal and genderless symbol of feminine intuition.

Sex Witch says

The Spell:

1. Understanding the true inclusive nature of the divine feminine is easier when we connect through moon energy. At night sit with a view of the moon. Have the Moon tarot card with you and a wineglass or goblet filled with red wine to represent blood or your nurturing beverage of choice. Pomegranate juice works great, too.

2. Simply sit enjoying your beverage and observing the power of the moon. Regardless of if we have menstrual cycles or not, we all cycle. Everyone has lows and highs, periods of wins and those of loss. The moon teaches us that the only constant is change. It comforts us to think that the wheel will turn when we're down and humbles us when we're up. The moon is mystery and intuition. It's the element water and emotion. It's annoyingly empathetic. The insecure fear the moon and darkness. Sip from your goblet, a cup containing nourishment, and feel the silver power of moonlight shine upon you.

3. Hold the Moon tarot card. The image may vary depending on your deck, but they all invoke a mysterious power. Creatures look to this life force for comfort. The moon gives back with a mysterious intuition but remembers to leave some wine in her goblet for herself. Don't push, just glance upon the card, and let her secrets reveal themselves to you. Like the moon and the tides, feminine motion occurs from within.

4. When you finish your drink or whenever you're ready, thank the divine feminine for her illuminating, frightening, empathetic, and intuitive power.

Tap into the Divine Masculine

You will need: A knife or ritual dagger and a tarot deck

The best time to cast the spell: During the day

> *Other times in our life call for action-oriented masculine energy. Stop associating masculine energy with douchenozzles and start associating it with action, ambition, and the force of will. Using the sun, the Sun card, a ritual dagger (it's not a bad idea to have one, but a knife works too), and the Magician card, this ritual invites all witches to tap into their divine masculine side.*

The Spell:

1. Sit somewhere where the sun can shine upon you. Masculine energy is not just for those with bio penises. Bright golden power shines and thrives within all of us. The sun transforms seeds into plants and provides for the Earth. It represents action. While the divine feminine works from within, the sun manifests outwardly, transforming desires into reality through power and hard work. Let the sun fall upon your face and know such powerful energy resides within you.

2. Look upon your knife or dagger. What makes a dagger a ritual dagger is that it's only used for magickal purposes. While any knife will do, objects can collect energy like debris, so it's good to have one solely for magickal purposes. Yes, knives are dangerous. I trust you can meditate upon the

power a knife wields without hurting yourself or others. Keep it next to you as a reminder of the strong penetrative force we all contain.

3. With the sun on your face and your knife by your side, stare at the Sun tarot card. This is the source of the power that fuels the Magician. The divine masculine is not afraid to shine brightly, ask for what it wants, and bask in its glory. The divine masculine is not afraid to take and burn others if needed. It's a bit arrogant but can back it up. The sun doesn't doubt that it deserves the world. In fact, it knows that the world depends upon it.

4. Meditate upon the fact that you not only deserve what you want, but that you have the power to manifest it, and are stronger than those who stand in your way. Such magickal swagger is not solely for cishet white men—but for every one of us.

Magick Masturbation

You will need: Yourself, a sex toy (optional)

The best time to cast the spell: The full moon

> ❝ *Sex magick is using sexual energy, in particular orgasms, to get what you want. It's most frequently done alone to minimize potential interference from pesky partners. This spell teaches sex magick through mastur-bation. No tools are needed unless you prefer to mastur-bate with a sex toy.*

Sex
Witch
says

The Spell:

1. Identify your intention. Sex magick does not have to have an intentional or even romantic goal in mind. It's often most

powerful when used for professional gain. For instance, perhaps you want a book deal, a raise, or another professional or monetary accomplishment. Meditate upon your will. Visualization is a powerful witch tool.

2. In bed or in the bath—wherever feels right—begin to pleasure yourself. Think about your intention, see your visualization, but it's okay if your mind wanders to erotic imagery to help achieve arousal.

3. Feel the sexual energy pulsate through your body. It is sacred. Enjoy it building throughout your body, filling you with pleasure and power.

4. If orgasms aren't an experience that comes easy to you, focus on directing the sexual fire toward your goal.

5. If you come, come hard. Let go. Give your body permission to release sexual energy with force. As you come, turn your mind to your intention. Visualize it into reality. You're at your book launch looking fabulous. Your bank account is higher than it's ever been. As your body lights up with orgasm, see your desire as reality.

6. Your orgasm is your command. Relax for as long as you like in the afterglow.

Banish Body Insecurity

You will need: A human figure candle, a bathtub, bath salts

Sex Witch says

The best time to cast the spell: The waning moon

❝ *There is no denying that we live in a society that inflicts impossible beauty standards and prizes certain bodies over others. However, as a witch, a rebel, it is helpful to understand the grandness of your own beauty and fight against the forces that would prefer you feel shame. You're hot, and this spell will help remove voices that say otherwise.*

The Spell:

1. Meditate while holding your human figure-shaped candle. Hold it tight in your hands. Visualize all the negative voices, the cruel thoughts, the mean things said, anything nasty and hurtful and untrue about your body flooding out of you and into the candle like a current. Take as long as you need.

2. When you are ready, take a deep breath and release. Place the candle on your altar or somewhere sacred and safe.

3. Light the candle.

4. Draw a bath. Stir in a good pour of bath salts. Occult shops sell banishing bath salts, but any will do.

5. Remove your clothes and get into the bath. Bath salts pull toxins, including the nasty body thoughts, out of you and into the water. Stay in the tub for as long as you like.

6. Get out. Watch the water swirl away, washing down body insecurities.

7. When the candle is finished burning, the spell is complete.

Smoking Sex Pot

You will need: Cannabis, damiana, roses, rolling papers or a pipe, a lighter, a bathtub, bath salts

The best time to cast the spell: Whenever you could use some self-care, relaxation, and a confidence boost

Confidence is sexy. Confidence is magick. It's the secret ingredient in attractiveness. When you're confident, you demand to be treated like an insanely hot person. You must treat yourself beautifully before you expect anyone else to. Curate confidence and self-love with this psychoactive self-love spell.

The Spell:

1. Obtain your cannabis flower. If you don't indulge in marijuana, you may skip this step. Other herbs that are handy in this spell include damiana, a known aphrodisiac, which can be purchased online or at your local apothecary. Dried crushed rose petals also mix wonderfully with cannabis. You can buy organic dried rose petals online or create your own. To dry your own roses, buy a bouquet. Do what thou wilt, but know that depending on the source of the roses, some petals may contain pesticides. Tie a string tightly around the stems of the bouquet and hang them upside down somewhere away from direct sunlight. In a week or less the petals will be ready.

2. Using your grinder or mortar and pestle, mix the cannabis, damiana, and rose petals. The cannabis calms and expands your mind, the damiana awakens your sexuality, and the rose petals welcome love. Pack a bowl or roll a spliff with your creation. As you blend and roll the herbs, chant: "I am hot as hell. I am hot as hell. I am hot as hell. Invoked from within, so others can tell, I am hot as hell."

3. Run yourself a hot bath. Fill it with bath salts of your choosing. Feel free to add rose petals so you may soak in rose tea. The salts will suck away toxins including insecure thoughts.

4. Lower yourself into the tub. Feel the pleasure of the warm water against your skin. Keep a lighter and your packed pipe or rolled spliff nearby.

5. Get high. You don't need an excuse. Pleasure is stigmatized by church and state to help keep us in line, but there's nothing wrong with feeling good. Enjoy the bath. Enjoy your magick herbal love mix. Shortening the magick words to "I am hot," or feel free to create your own, affirm your attractiveness over and over until your bathwater becomes cool and your spliff is gone. You can do this anytime you like.

Fuck Off Facebook

You will need: Your electronics, salt, a small container (a 4-ounce mason jar is ideal), a Sharpie, a bold attitude

The best time to cast the spell: During the waning moon

> " *We know from our own social media activity that what we post is not always a fair reflection of how we feel inside. As a result, it's easy to stalk an ex or someone with great influence over our emotions only to feel badly about ourselves. Use this spell to banish insecurity created through social media and encourage confidence when we use our devices.*

Sex Witch says

The Spell:

1. Unfollow your ex or the person making you feel shitty. Blocking them is even better. If for whatever reason, such as professional standing, that's not an option, hit the mute button. Unfollow and mute their family and close friends. If it makes you feel better, send a message that explains you need to unfriend them but hope to connect in the future.

2. It's unrealistic for most of us not to use electronics or social media. However, we want them to lift us up. Pick an image of something or someone who makes you feel confident and set it as your wallpaper.

3. Create your own magickal salts to use in protective and banishing work. If you can obtain salt with special meaning—for instance mine is from Iceland—all the better. However, any salt will do. Pour it into its own container; a 4-ounce mason jar works great. Write a symbol of love and strength, such as a simple heart, on the lid with the Sharpie.

4. Sprinkle the salt in front of your door and around your home to banish negativity and usher in joy. Do not re-follow those hurting you until the emotional response they provoke dies out.

Curate Community; Create a Coven

You will need: Trusted fellow witches and a place to meet

The best time to cast the spell: Begin organizing at any minute and meet at each Sabbat, or witch's holiday, which commemorates the changing seasons.

Sex Witch says

    ❝ *Friends and support systems outside of romantic and sexual relationships are crucial for our mental health. They prevent us from looking to our partner to meet all of our needs, which will end in failure. Magickally speaking, while having a solitary practice is crucial, a coven helps us grow both our support system and practice. A coven gives us an opportunity to practice ritual and ceremonial magick while connecting us to community and the sabbaths.*

The Spell:

1. Call upon your fellow trusted witches. Who do you want in your coven? Who can you trust? What can each witch bring to the table? Be inclusive yet discriminate. Avoid inviting those who are flaky or don't take magick seriously.

2. Pick a name for your coven. What words invoke the power you wish to manifest?

3. Create a secure email chain to organize. To start, meet each witch's Sabbat. Allow a different witch to lead each meeting so everyone gets an opportunity to express themselves and teach the rest a new perspective on the changing of the seasons. Devising a ritual may involve asking the rest to bring flowers, items to be charged upon the altar, or poems or writings that invoke the essence of the holiday. Before the official coven meeting starts, it's a good idea to bring snacks and beverages so the coven has time to hang out and bond before ritual.

4. Each meeting should begin by casting a circle. What happens at coven stays at coven.

5. While coven meetings can remain secret, support your sisters outside of ritual in daily life.

What the Hell Do I Want?

You will need: A journal, pen, tarot cards

The best time to cast the spell: When you're confused and horny

> 66 *We can't bring our kinky sex fantasy or dream partner to life if we're unsure of what we want. This spell reveals the truth of your will, so you may take action to manifest it.*

Sex
Witch
says

The Spell:

1. Open your journal to a blank page. As messy as possible, begin scribbling down what you want. Do you want to meet a partner who shares the same level of professional enthusiasm and isn't allergic to cats so you can one day move in together and hit power couple status? Or do you want to get your brains fucked out by someone hot and sweaty but totally unsuitable for long-term companionship? Both are spiritual experiences, and neither is wrong. The only "wrong" is not following your heart's—or genitals'—desire.

2. Eventually, no matter what you wrote in the first sentence, your journaling will reveal the truth.

3. Take your tarot cards. Hold the deck and ask, "What do I truly need right now?" Shuffle the cards until you feel finished, and then pick out a single card to represent your needs. For instance, once shortly after a breakup when I was ready for sex but not a serious relationship, I got the three of cups, a card of great joy and abundance. Coupled with my journaling, I knew I needed fun sex and to simply enjoy life for a moment.

4. Go forth and manifest your will!

Flames for Courage

You will need: A cauldron, a pen and paper, a lighter

The best time to cast the spell: Nighttime during the waning moon

> *The world can put us down. However, often we're the ones holding ourselves back, even if we can't see it. For example, with all my writing about sex, drugs, and*

witchcraft have I made myself completely un-wifeable? Or am I fucking awesome and too interesting for anyone so aligned with mainstream society? When we doubt ourselves, our insecurities can become self-fulfilling prophecies. Let's burn those bad thoughts away and step into bravery.

Sex
Witch
says

The Spell:

1. You will need a firesafe cauldron, which can be bought online or at your local occult store.

2. Using a pen and paper, write down all of your self-doubts, insecurities, and anything that affects your ability to feel confident and courageous.

3. Hold your paper, light a corner, and drop it into the cauldron. Make sure to practice fire safety. Keep a window open so smoke doesn't set off fire alarms, keep a fire extinguisher nearby, and never leave a flame unattended.

4. Watch it burn. Stare into the flames. The same fire exists within your heart and is ready for the world to see.

5. When the paper of fear is all burnt up, collect the ashes and sprinkle them at a crossroads.

Bedroom Blessing

You will need: Your muggle cleaning supplies, water, a pot, one bay leaf, sea salt, pepper, dried basil, cloves, Florida Water, vinegar, a mason jar or other container, one lemon, eucalyptus essential oil, cheesecloth

The best time to cast the spell: The new moon

Sex Witch says

❝ *Cleaning is crucial, but trust me, even with my Virgo moon I rarely enjoy it. Beyond lingering bad energy there's the simple fact that humans shed skin cells. Your former lovers are all over your bedroom like cat hair. Use this magickal floor wash containing ingredients hailed for their purification properties after cleaning muggle-style to remove energy and DNA left behind by past partners to usher in new love.*

The Spell:

1. Clean your floors using a broom, mop, or a whole lot of Swiffer-ing. Focus on the bedroom but get your entire home or apartment. Not only does this scrub away unwanted ex DNA, but a floor wash is just gross on a dirty floor.

2. Add two cups of water, ideally filtered or spring water, into a pot. Add one bay leaf, ¼ cup of sea salt, seven twists of pepper, one tablespoon of dried basil, and a tablespoon of cloves. Cover and turn the heat to high until it reaches a boil. Reduce heat to low and let simmer for ten minutes.

3. While the herbal water is simmering, add ½ cup of Florida Water and ½ cup vinegar to your mason jar.

4. Add the juice of one lemon using a strainer to keep seeds out.

5. Add 3 ml of eucalyptus essential oil.

6. After ten minutes, turn off the stove and let the herbal mixture cool. Your senses will be alive with the smells of your kitchen witchery.

7. Once cool, strain the herbal water and add it to the mason jar. Screw the lid on tightly and shake to combine.

8. Using a mop, washcloth, or spray bottle, cleanse your floors with your magickal floor wash in a counterclockwise direction.

Sexuality Acceptance Spell

You will need: Your own dirty underwear, rose quartz, ribbon

The best time to cast the spell: When you want to summon good kinky love

> 66 *Kink-shaming is an epidemic! People mistake a love of verbal humiliation for a desire to be treated shitty outside of the bedroom or think that an interest in sex parties makes you some kind of undesirable creep! But deep down, those who judge us are misunderstood, sexually repressed muggles. Use this pervy ritual to remind yourself that as long as your fantasies are between two consenting adults, there's nothing wrong with you and you deserve to experience them.*

Sex Witch says

The Spell:

1. Cloth dolls are often used to create a poppet, or a human-like figure meant to represent a person. However, making one requires sewing skills, which not all witches possess. Cloth dolls also come primarily from African magickal traditions, and with so much cultural appropriation going on, I figured we'd try something different. So grab your dirty underwear. If that doesn't show the spirits your presence, I don't know what will. Psst . . . bodily fluids are extremely powerful.

2. Unfold your underwear. Don't be embarrassed! Embrace your beautiful body. Place your rose quartz, which is charged with self-love, in the middle of your underwear. Wrap them around the crystal.

3. Use your ribbon to tie up your rose underwear into a nice little package, while saying, "My kinks are normal; I am hot. I banish shame; and tie this knot."

4. Hold it in your hands. Using your powers of visualization—one of the most important skills a witch should have—see yourself living out your dirtiest sexual fantasies with an ideal and accepting partner.

5. Place your pretty package on your love altar or somewhere safe and keep it there for a week.

See Your Ex Clearly

You will need: A scrying mirror

The best time to cast the spell: When you're ready to move on

Sometimes we sugarcoat memories, placing our exes on pedestals and remembering only their positive traits. This makes it easy to get trapped in nostalgia. We don't have to demonize our exes; however, if you're stuck in good memories and struggling to move on, it's helpful to remember the full picture, including their negative traits.

The Spell:

1. Sit in a meditation pose holding your scrying mirror. Scrying mirrors are typically black and made out of materials such as obsidian. If you have a crystal ball, that works too. If obtaining a scrying mirror is difficult or out of your budget, you can use a small mirror or other reflective surface. However, ideally the mirror should only be used for scrying.

2. Close your eyes and think of your ex. It's okay if pain, regret, love, or any other difficult emotions arise. These must be felt in order to move on.

3. Begin mentally listing their negative traits. Perhaps underneath their appeal they are selfish, manipulative, and dishonest. Be as brutal as you want.

4. Open your eyes and look into your scrying mirror. Chant "Mirror, mirror, illuminating star, show me [insert ex's name] for who they are."

5. Sit looking into the mirror. Eventually it will show you something. It may not look like a movie of them acting cruelly; once during this exercise I simply received a mental download alerting me that an ex was a massive liar with many secrets. Be open to whatever comes.

6. When you are finished, set down the scrying mirror. Take a few cleansing breaths.

7. Do something nice for yourself—like have a sweet or spend time with your pet—to recover from a difficult exercise.

Break Toxic Cycles

You will need: A pen and paper, black rope or string, scissors, a firesafe container, a lighter or handheld blowtorch

The best time to cast the spell: During the waning or new moon

> Most of us need to conquer our demons at some point in order to break from unhealthy patterns or partner selection stemming from trauma. This spell uses a cord-cutting ritual to help us identify and end old patterns, so we may cut that shit out and love and fuck from a healthy place of confidence.

Sex Witch says

The Spell:

1. Most people are assholes. But sometimes we keep letting assholes into our assholes—I mean life! Let's cut that shit out—literally. Using your pen and paper, list your unhealthy patterns that lead to toxic cycles. For instance, I wrote: "Moving too fast, ignoring red flags, and expecting people to change." These must go!

2. Sit down and cut about a yard of black string—or more depending on how many patterns you want to break. State your crime out loud as you tie a knot in the rope. "I move too fast in relationships," knot! "I ignore red flags," knot! And so on.

3. Once you've gone through your entire list, tie the ends of the rope to form a loop.

4. Gently place the circle of rope over your hands like shackles. Feel the toxicity. Consider how each pattern plays into the other forming a loop.

5. Cut the rope with your scissors in between each knot, breaking the chain one snip after the other. Bye! Bye-bye! As you cut, state: "I release myself from the cycle holding me back."

6. When you are finished, put the ends of the rope in the firesafe container, light it, and watch it burn. When your unhealthy patterns are all burnt up, throw out the remains and take out the trash immediately.

Green Flying Ointment

You will need: 1 cup of ground cannabis flower; a grinder or mortar and pestle; 1 cup of coconut oil; a medium-size bowl;

a dash of water; a slow cooker; double boiler; or saucepan; a strainer or cheesecloth; a container such as a mason jar

The best time to cast the spell: Whenever you're ready to get your hands dirty and elevate to another plane of existence

> 66 *Tap into your inner kitchen witch to create your own flying ointment—a potion historically inserted into the vagina for hallucinogenic effects. Flying ointment exists primarily for the simple yet crucial task of having a good time while masturbating. The psychedelic properties offer personal insight and clarity. This recipe is modified to replace difficult to obtain and poisonous ingredients such as deadly nightshade with cannabis for a safer and easier to procure experience.*

Sex Witch says

The Spell:

1. You will need to buy some weed. Your favorite strains work; so does low-grade shake to save money. Grind up your cannabis using a grinder or a mortar and pestle to a nice smooth crumble, or the consistency you would use to make a joint. It should be fine (like you) but not so fine that it slips through a cheesecloth or strainer.

2. Combine your cup of ground cannabis and cup of coconut oil in your medium-size bowl. Add a splash or two of water (this helps prevent burning).

3. As some of us found out in high school, you can't just shove a bud into your mouth, chew, and expect to get high. You have to decarb the weed. Decarboxylation uses heat to activate the THC. This process happens on its own through smoking, but when creating oils and edibles, we have to take another step. If you're using a slow cooker, pour in the mixture, then set the slow cooker on low for eight hours. Stir periodically. If you're

using a double boiler, add the mixture then cook for six to eight hours, stirring frequently. If you're using a saucepan, add your mixture and cook on low for at least three hours, frequently stirring, as this way has the highest chance of burning. Don't be afraid to add a little more water if the pot looks like it's burning.

4. Congrats on decarbing your weed! You're a stoner witch now. Place your strainer or cheesecloth over your mason jar. Pour your cannabis oil through and into the jar.

5. Let it cool. Store it in a cool dark place up to two months or in the freezer for up to three months.

6. Your final product is your cannabis flying oil. You can drizzle it on food or replace any muggle oil with it to make edibles. To use it as a tincture, simply pour it into a tincture bottle. Eating it will produce the most psychoactive effects. However, witches with a vagina can also use it as lube and masturbate with it. Because the mucous membranes are different on penises, you need a consenting vagina or anus to use flying lube. Do not use it with condoms as oil degrades latex and witches have safe sex.

7. If applied vaginally, the flying ointment will increase blood flow and orgasm. It also decreases pain without numbing you out. Apply it while practicing sex magick for added abilities. Witches do not demonize the psychoactive properties of plants. Cannabis is medicine, and in addition to increasing pleasure when applied topically, smoking or ingesting cannabis can heighten our creative states and psychic abilities. There's no hard-and-fast rule for how to use your flying ointment. It is very safe to experiment with, as you cannot overdose on cannabis. Use your flying ointment however best fits your needs while listening to your intuition.

Feel Hot as Fuck

You will need: Red lipstick, a mirror, music, cannabis or wine (optional), your makeup collection

The best time to cast this spell: Whenever the hell you want

> 66 *It is an evil, virulent, muggle lie that wanting to feel pretty is a bad thing! Yes, you are worthy of love and fuckable all of the time. But glamour is more than a magazine. The word used to refer to spellcasting. But beauty is as powerful as ever. Use this mantra makeup ritual to feel hot as fuck.*

Sex Witch says

The Spell:

1. Take a moment to meditate. Close your eyes and enjoy a few deep inhales and exhales. How do you want to feel? It doesn't matter how far-out it sounds. You can manifest it. For instance, go with, "I am terrifyingly hot." This is your mantra.

2. Using red lipstick—red for fire, lust, and love—write your mantra across the top of the mirror you use to do your makeup.

3. Put on music that makes you feel powerful. If you like, indulge in some wine or cannabis. As long as we don't harm ourselves or others, witches know there is nothing wrong with psychoactive substances, just like there's nothing wrong with feeling hot.

4. Take out your makeup. Boldly and carefully apply it in the mirror. Follow your instinct with color, shapes, and styles.

5. Go forth and be hot. Repeat your mantra in your mind as needed.

4. Magick for Seduction

Magick for seduction aids us in manifesting our desires, from enchanting lovers to safely stepping into our own sexual power. Many witches warn against using magick to bend the will of another. Well, these witches are often liars. Oh my god, come on, everyone wants someone to be obsessed with them! We think with our genitals and then our hearts. We're all animals—let's just admit that we're here to get laid. While certain seduction spells should be done with caution, we also must remember that we perform seduction spells every day, from selfies to a spritz of perfume. You cannot force love or sex; you can only encourage the universe to bend in your favor to speed up what will happen naturally. Tap into such power with the following seduction spells.

Summon the Perfect Partner

You will need: Pen and paper; a red, pink, or white candle shaped like a penis, vagina, male or female figure; a condom (optional); lube; a candle-carving tool; your favorite variety of love oil

The best time to cast the spell: The waxing moon

> 66 *This spell is some real fucking witchcraft combining candle magick and sex magick. You're going to fuck a candle and summon your dream partner. Hold tight and be careful what you wish for—it just might come true.*

Sex
Witch
says

The Spell:

1. What do you want in a partner? Someone who fucks your brains out? A daddy who pays for everything? Someone non-judgmental? Kind? Kinky? Be honest! Write down exactly what you're looking for and be honest. Satan knows when you're lying.

2. Grab your candle, which should represent the person you wish to conjure. Whether that's a penis candle, a pussy candle, a man or woman figure is up to you. Remember that these candle shapes are just representations of energy, and you can use any candle for any gender. Red represents passion; pink more self-love; and white is a stand-in color. If you intend to penetrate yourself with the candle, a penis shape does work best.

3. Live with the candle for seven days as if it were your partner. Have it sit next to you while you watch TV. Let it sleep in your bed.

4. If you like, using a condom and lots of lube as to not get wax in any orifice, have penetrative sex with the candle. Perform sex magick while the candle is inside of you. While you fuck yourself, visualize them coming to life.

5. After seven days, using your candle-carving tool, carve your name and zodiac symbol into the candle.

6. Anoint the candle with your love oil of choice. Place the candle on your love altar.

7. Light it and let that baby burn. When the candle is finished burning, the spell is complete.

Why Are You So Obsessed with Me?

You will need: A pair of panties, La Flamme Oil, confidence

The best time to cast the spell: Before a date and sexy sleepover

> 66 *La Flamme is an obsession oil that many witches warn against. Why? Because it's powerful and the very definition of "be careful what you wish for." It's so powerful that it has a mind of its own! Once I attended a La Flamme–making class and got the stuff all over me. I had intended to use it on this lovely Libra lady I was seeing. But that night, I had a breakup date with this awful Taurus man and ended up fucking him! And then I couldn't get rid of the guy. Anyway, the lesson here is to use La Flamme with caution. You can buy some online or at your local occult store. The rest of the spell is fueled by confidence and even more powerful.*

Sex Witch says

The Spell:

1. Meditate on how awesome you are. List of all the great things about you. Don't stop. Let your ego swell for miles. There's nothing wrong with ego. The worst people in the world get away with murder because they have massive egos. It's about time more witches became confident of their power in this world. Whoever is the object of your obsession spell is a lucky motherfucker.

2. It's glamour magick time! Put on your favorite outfit, hair accessories, makeup, and whatever makes you feel like the greatest incarnation of yourself.

3. Wear underwear that is sexy, but that you are okay with getting rid of. You're going to leave it in your lover's home.

4. If you are using La Flamme, dab a little bit behind your ears and on your panties. By the way, your panties should get messy and smell like you. The dirtier the better! If you don't want to use La Flamme, stick with your signature perfume or scent.

5. Go out. Be confident. If at any time you feel insecure, just remember that you are absolutely fine without this loser (this holds true even if they are not a loser).

6. After the fuck fest, leave behind your panties. Your lover will smell them and be totally obsessed with you. And keep that confidence up!

Feel Insanely Hot

You will need: A red candle, love oil or some bodily fluids, a lighter, your favorite music, a place to dance naked

The best time to cast the spell: At night during the full moon

Sex Witch says

 The world does not want you to know how powerful you are. The world does not want you to know that you can weaponize your sexuality before it's weaponized against you. Your body and your desires are yours. Pleasure should not be prosecuted. This spell couples sex magick with a candle ritual and music to make sure you're fully aware of how hot you are—and ready to use such power to get what you want. When the patriarchy punishes and silences us for our sexuality, there is great power and honor in using it to our advantage.

The Spell:

1. Anoint your red candle. You may use any love oil, or ideally, vaginal or seminal fluids.

2. Dim the rest of the lights in your home, and light other candles if needed. The atmosphere should feel feral. Ensure a clear view of the full moon.

3. Put on music that invokes your animal nature. When in doubt, go for "Closer" by Nine Inch Nails.

4. Strip off your clothes. Dance until you sweat. Your intention is to become aware of your sacred sexuality.

5. As your candle burns, just dance and move naturally. You should feel your power stirring in the base of your spine and uncurling up your back like a serpent. This is your primal energy. Remember it and tap into it whenever you need.

Baby Gay Blessing

You will need: A purse or other bag you can carry around with you, a condom or dental dam, lube packets, a travel pillbox, makeup-removing wipes, your favorite edible treat, a relaxing place to meditate

The best time to cast the spell: When you want to celebrate yourself

> ❝ Hex yeah, queer witches, congrats on coming out. Now is an exciting time. You get to change your Tinder settings and pretentiously come out to all your boring straight high school friends. Or you can keep it your secret. There are no rules. You come out however you feel like it to whoever you please. You make the rules. Perhaps today you identify as bisexual and queer, but in a year you'll identify as gay. It doesn't matter. All that matters is that you feel supported, magickal, safe, and powerful.

Sex Witch says

The Spell:

1. Just in case you do end up wanting queer sex, as a modern witch, you need a go bag. This can be a purse or something you keep in your pocket. Add and subtract as needed, but it should contain protection—and I don't mean black tourmaline. Carry condoms and a dental dam, and if you have trouble finding a dental dam, you can make one out of a condom by cutting it to form a square. Carry lube, because sex is always better with lube, especially if you're playing with the ass, as the rectum doesn't lubricate naturally. That doesn't mean we shouldn't put things in it—sodomy is saintly—it just means it needs some extra attention. The butthole is a diva. Bring your meds so you don't have withdrawal at a sleepover. Carry makeup-removing wipes to protect your skin regardless of whose bed you're in.

2. Now it's time to pick out your Queer Patron Saint. Mine are David Bowie and Freddie Mercury, my two spiritual fathers. They look over me, I have saint candles of them from Etsy on my altar, and I listen to their songs for strength. Hecate, Lucifer, Dionysus, Aphrodite, and Venus are all grand, but sometimes you just need Bowie as your higher power. To pick your Queer Patron Saint, simply pick a living or dead queer icon who makes you feel proud to be yourself. Meditate on their influence over you. Pull that strength into your heart. You can always tap into their energy whenever you need strength.

3. Finally, please have a slice of cake, cookie, or whatever your favorite baked treat is. Coming out is very challenging, but it's one of the greatest things you'll ever do. There are

hard times ahead, but nothing compared to the joy and plea-sure. So have your cake and eat it too.

Venus Powder

You will need: A mortar and pestle, dragon's blood, a dried red rose, flour, a mixing bowl, red glitter, vanilla extract, red food dye (optional), pubic hair clippings (optional), your signature perfume, small containers

The best time to cast the spell: Whenever you're not afraid to get messy for love

> ❝ *Follow this Venus Powder recipe to create a magickal powder to sprinkle around your lover's home, rub on candles, or use in whatever creative way you come up with to ensure they stay enthralled by you.*

Sex Witch says

The Spell:

1. Using your mortar and pestle, grind up seven pieces of dragon's blood. Dragon's blood is not only associated with Venus but used to amplify spells. It is the resin of a palm plant and has long been employed as a red dye. Red is the color of love and lust. As you are crushing the dragon's blood, and for the rest of this spell, think about the lover you wish to attract, the relationship you want, whatever your intention is behind creating this love powder.

2. Take one dried red rose and crush it up. I find it useful to keep bouquets of dried red roses around the house for spell-casting. Mix the crushed rose with the dragon's blood.

3. Put ¼ cup of flour in a mixing bowl to act as your base. Add the dragon's blood, dried rose, and as much red glitter as

you please. The glitter adds sparkle and is nearly impossible to remove, which is a win for us and too bad for the object of our spellcasting.

4. Add a few dashes of vanilla extract.

5. If you like, add some red food coloring to increase the color magick. If food dyes aren't for you, skip it.

6. Likewise, for extra potency you can put in a few trims of your pubic hair. If this grosses you out or you find it offensive to sprinkle public hair around your lover's home without their knowledge, skip this step.

7. Spray a spritz of your signature perfume into the powder.

8. The recipe does not have to be exact. Eyeball the ingredients and trust your intuition. When you are finished, place the powder in jars or a baggie. You can anoint love candles with it, sprinkle it around your lover's home, put some on top of a picture of them or the tarot card that represents their zodiac sign, or even sprinkle some on their body when they're not looking.

The Scarlet Soak

You will need: A bathtub, bath salts, a glittery bath bomb (optional)

The best time to cast the spell: The new moon

Sex Witch says

When sexual shame is as ingrained as it is in our society, even the most sexually confident of us feel badly sometimes. Whether it was biting words from our parents or the bullying of classmates, labels are hard to scrub off. But thankfully, there's a spell for

*that. Your bathtub is a giant cauldron. Wash away any
societally ingrained hang-ups and soak in the power
of the sexually liberated goddess to free the sacred slut
within you.*

The Spell:

1. Fix yourself the most luxurious bath. Fill it with cleansing
bath salts, but also any fabulous bath bombs or potions your
heart desires. You are the master of your body and this bath
cauldron; you get to decide what goes in it.

2. Once the tub is filled, lie back. You are not washing off
your sins because they do not exist. You are perfect as you
are. You are letting the salt and water suck out any harsh
words, names, labels, and experiences that you and your
body have been put through. Perhaps it is name-calling from
an abusive ex. Perhaps it is shame-riddled teachings of your
family or religious figures. Maybe you were bullied in school
or continue to be bullied online. It's okay to go to the dark
place. You are safe, and the magick bathwaters are drawing
all that past negativity and shame out of you.

3. Enjoy the hot bath for as long as you want, and when
you're ready, as you're in control, pull the drain and let any
nasty residue of ill-informed—and probably jealous—others
swirl away.

Come to Me Candied Rose Petals

You will need: Two large egg whites, a whisk, a bowl, a pastry
brush, petals from organic two roses, ½ cup of sugar

The best time to cast the spell: The waxing moon

There are (true) witch rumors about baking cakes filled with menstrual blood or other additives meant to enchant a lover gullible enough to eat it. Baking is not for everyone. However, candied rose petals are supermagickal and even the most anti-kitchen witch can make them. For those who love baking, add these candied rose petals as decoration to your favorite cake recipe. I suggest a Persian Love Cake (Venus adores Persian Love Cakes).

The Spell:

1. Whisk the egg whites in a mixing bowl until fluffy and foamy.

2. Paint each organic (so there are no pesticides) rose petal with egg white on both sides.

3. Sprinkle on both sides with sugar. As you do, whisper to the roses, "I am loved."

4. Leave them out on a dry stick rack overnight. They taste like a rose smells. Eat one yourself, feed it to a lover, or use them to decorate cakes and other treats.

First Date Blessing

You will need: Your favorite song, cannabis or wine (optional), makeup, string, one red rose petal, black tourmaline, a snippet of your hair

The best time to cast the spell: Before the first date

First dates are so exciting! Yes, you could meet someone who shows up drunk and spends the whole date ranting about their ex, but at least you got out there! In all seriousness, though, first dates get a bad rap, but are superfun, whether or not you meet the person of your

dreams. Why? It's a chance for you to shine, baby. Get out of the house and let the world see you sparkle. Cast this spell to find love while protecting yourself from any monsters out there.

The Spell:

1. Put on your favorite song or even better put on a whole damn playlist that reminds you how fuckable you are.

2. If you like, partake in some cannabis or wine. Not enough to get messed up, but enough to let loose.

3. Do your hair and makeup in a manner that makes you feel extremely good about yourself.

4. Place a piece of string in front of you and on it put one fresh petal off a red rose. In the middle of the petal, place a small chunk of black tourmaline, which is a stone that contains protective powers. Snip just a teeny bit of your hair, just enough to sprinkle on top of your bundle. Tie up the bundle with the string and put it into your purse or pocket. It's there with you all night.

Deal with Your Demons

You will need: The Devil tarot card, the Death tarot card, a pen and notebook

The best time to cast the spell: The waning moon

> ❝ *Do not fear the Devil. If you look at the two human figures in the Rider-Waite Devil card, they have shackles around their necks, but the chains are loose enough to remove. This is how we must approach our own demons keeping us back from love. Underneath our demons are devilish, beautiful, consensual kinky desires*

Sex
Witch
says

we deserve to have. Just as the Devil is your friend, so is Death, and the two enjoy a beautiful dance together. Death need not mean a literal death, but rather a transformation or rebirth. Follow this meditation to kill your demons and make friends with your dope dark side. The power of visualization is one of the most potent tools a witch can master.

The Spell:

1. Sit somewhere conducive to meditation. Hold the Devil card in your hand. If you stare into tarot cards, they often reveal truths. What personal demons are holding you back? Jot anything down that comes to mind.

2. What are your demons? Is it insecurity? What does that monster look like? Close your eyes and visualize all your demons in creature form. Perhaps insecurity is a clammy gray vampiric demon. (Mentally) grab your weapon of choice. Mine is a knife and sword; yours can be anything. Within your meditation, kill your demons.

3. Open your eyes and gaze upon the Death card. Think about rebirth. What does this card whisper to you?

4. Close your eyes and return to your mental war zone. Like a phoenix, watch yourself rise from the ashes of your demons. With insecurity—or whatever the name of your demon may be—dead, what powerful being can you be now?

5. Open your eyes. Your demons are dead. You are reborn stronger than ever. Do not underestimate the power of visualization.

A Ritual for Just Sex

You will need: A pen and paper, string or rope, scissors

The best time to cast the spell: Anytime you desire casual sex with someone

> 66 *Sometimes we are only interested in a sexual rela-*
> *tionship and wish to avoid a romantic obligation.*
> *Ensure that your hookup is no strings attached with this*
> *ritual. It uses literal pieces of string and a reflection on*
> *what healthy hookups are and how to communicate your*
> *desires to the other party.*

Sex Witch says

The Spell:

1. Divide a piece of paper into three columns. The left column is for pros, the right column is for cons, and the middle column is how you will merge the two in order to create a realistic compromise to ensure an emotionally, spiritually, and physically satisfying experience.

2. Write down the pros. Remember that just because sex is casual doesn't mean it can't be fulfilling or emotionally intimate. Perhaps pros of having sex with this person are that it will feel good to be fucked. It's a bonding experience; it can fill your needs without too much time demands; etc.

3. Write down the cons. There is the risk of catching feelings. If this is someone you're already friends with, the relationship could change.

4. In the middle column write down how you plan to mitigate the pros and cons. Think of this as your solution column. For instance, you can write things such as "communication" and "honesty" to help you express your sexual needs while considering emotional fallout.

5. Take out your string. Cut three pieces total, for the length of each column.

6. Braid them together. This is symbolic of using your will and knowledge to mitigate any potential problems and infuse the good with the bad to craft sacred realistic expectations for the experience.

5. Magick for Sex

Pleasure is your birthright. You deserve hot, consensual sex. It does not have to fit the molds of heterosexual expectations, and you can undoubtedly fuck to come rather than conceive. While sex is often deemed silly or unimportant compared to other political issues, this couldn't be further from the truth. How and who you can fuck is always one of the first things regulated by the government. We see this through the attack on reproductive and LGBTQIA+ rights. It sometimes appears that the white men in charge are only interested in protecting their pleasure. Witches cannot stand for this.

The following sex spells combine scientific sex ed with occult knowledge to teach you how to create a sigil for sexual pleasure, adequately prepare for anal sex, and unleash your inner kinks. We will also pray for sex positivity and do our part to make the world more welcoming to all. In contrast to patriarchal traditions, many pagan and ancient traditions revere the kinky and the queer. It's no coincidence that interest in both witchcraft and sex positivity skyrocketed among the general public as politics become more hateful and controlling. We don't want to be regulated and told who and how we can fuck. Sex is an expression of love or sometimes just an expression of lust—both can be healthy and healing. Use this chapter to drop the programmed shame and revel in pleasure.

A Prayer for Sex Positivity

You will need: Sage, a pink candle, the Empress tarot card, rose quartz, any other objects that represent what sex positivity means to you

The best time to cast the spell: The waxing moon

Sex Witch says

> *Sex positivity is the belief that enjoying consensual sex is a good thing, not something to be ashamed of. It rejects the sex-negative notion often perpetuated by church and state that sex should be between a married man and woman with the goal of procreation. It believes that pleasure is our right. Sex positivity denounces homophobia and believes that everyone has the right to love and sex regardless of orientation or gender. The movement also accepts alternative sexualities such as kink and polyamory. In a world in which people are still persecuted for their sexual identity, sex positivity needs all the help it can get. Cast this spell to offer protection to everyone fighting to be their authentic self and spread the message of sex positivity.*

The Spell:

1. As you sage your space, visualize the smoke clearing away outdated and hateful notions about sexuality.

2. Light a pink candle on your love altar. Pink is associated with love, but also care and compassion.

3. Place the Empress tarot card on your altar by the candle. The Empress, in her garden and embellished dress, represents fertility and abundance. She is connected to nature and proud of her sexuality. While she's depicted as a woman, this does not mean this card speaks exclusively

to women. The divine feminine is within all of us and, through this card, can represent loving acceptance of sexuality.

4. Feel free to get creative and enhance your altar with rose quartz or other items that represent sex positivity to you.

5. Meditate in front of your altar. Think about all the hate spewed by antiabortion activists, homophobic people, and anyone else who wishes to harm others simply for living a life true to their sexual identity. As you exhale, imagine that you are sending their hate back to them. Elaborate props are not always needed in spells. Your will is your most powerful asset.

6. Redirect your energy to positivity. As you breathe, imagine yourself living the sex life of your dreams, LGBTQIA+ folks loving freely, and kinky and poly people sharing their truth without judgment. Invoking the energy of the Empress, imagine blowing out magickal loving glitter with each exhale.

7. Say out loud, "May everyone fuck and love freely without threat of persecution. May everyone experience their right to pleasure. May those who wish to torment others fall on their own sword of hate."

8. Light the pink candle whenever you are home and repeat the meditation and incantation as desired. Set an example of sex positivity through your own life. It's your witch's duty.

Conjure a Sex Sigil

You will need: Pen and paper, a red candle, sage, honey, dried rose petals, an incense such as Venus or Attraction, a small plate or coaster, newspaper, a carving tool, oils such as

La Flamme Oil, Adam and Eve Oil, Aphrodite Oil, Pan Oil, Scarlette's Seduction Oil, Fire of Love Oil, glitter (optional)

The best time to cast the spell: Cast this spell during the waxing or full moon or whenever you're horny.

Sex Witch says

" *Everyone fucks differently. What does hot sex look like to you? What do you want? As long as what you want is consensual, you deserve it. Expedite your sex mission with candle magick and a sigil.*

The Spell:

1. Write a letter of intention. How do you want to get fucked? Who do you want to fuck you? What do you want out of the experience? Detail your desires in ink. Be as explicit as possible. Ideally, this spell would make a grandmother faint if she read it.

2. Boil your intention letter down to one concise and descriptive sentence.

3. Use that sentence to create a sigil.

4. Take your red candle in your hands. If you don't have red, white will do. Pullout candles are great for this spell. You can fill the glass it comes in with honey and incense.

5. Use sage to cleanse your candle.

6. If you have a pullout candle, remove it from the glass. Taste the honey and then squirt enough in the bottom to cover the surface. Sprinkle in some crushed rose petals. Light your incense and insert it into the glass as the smoke billows, with a flat surface such as a coaster on top to keep the smoke in. Set it aside.

7. Over the newspaper, carve your sigil into your candle. Add your name, zodiac symbol, and any other fun words such as "daddy" or "double-headed dildo."

8. Anoint the candle using one of the oils listed above or a simple love or attraction oil. Rose water also works, as do bodily fluids such as menstrual blood, vaginal fluid, or semen. Witches can't be judgy or squeamish.

9. If you're into glitter, pour some onto the newspaper. Red glitter works, as do other colors particular to your desire. If you want to find a sugar daddy, the green for money works. If you want to bring out more top-y energy, use gold to represent the sun and the divine masculine. Go wild and mix in some dried rose petals.

10. Roll the oiled-up candle into your glitter.

11. Carefully remove the coaster from the glass and plop the candle into its jar. Poof!

12. Set the candle on your love altar and light it. When the candle is finished burning, your spell is complete.

Slay a Play Party

You will need: Makeup, clothing, and lingerie that make you feel sexy; a mirror; a purse or small bag that you're comfortable carrying with you; condoms and barriers; lube; crystals such as red jasper, garnet; Venus Powder; your favorite perfume; protective stones such as black tourmaline

The best time to cast the spell: Cast this spell before going to a play party, witch.

Sex
Witch
says

Magickally, mirrors are often used for protec-
tion. Some say they are a portal from our world
to others. If witches feel under attack, they may draw
a protective sigil on the back of a mirror. However,
sometimes a mirror is just a mirror. In this spell, we
use a mirror in conjunction with glamour magick to
see ourselves in our full glory.

Before attending a play party, memorize the orga-
nization's code of conduct. Nonconsensual touching is
the number one no-no. Despite how scary sex parties
may sound, often such events are safer than traditional
parties as all those in attendance are well-versed in
consent. Legit ones will also have guardians present to
make sure everyone is safe and acting according to the
code of conduct.

Before you arrive set boundaries for yourself and
date, or if you're not bringing a date, consider bringing
a trusted friend so you're not alone. Your goal may be
to have a threesome, to have sex with your partner in
an erotic atmosphere, or to simply suss out the scene.
Setting goals and boundaries beforehand prevent you
from doing anything in the heat of the moment you
might regret later.

The Spell:

1. While following the dress code of the event, put on lingerie and clothing (layers are your friend) that make you feel like a powerful sex god(dess). Use colors such as a fiery red lipstick for passion or a silver necklace reminiscent of the mysterious moon to invoke the mood you wish to convey. It's okay to approach clothing and makeup as costume and war paint.

2. Look at yourself in your mirror. Close your eyes. Use your power to remove ego. When you open your eyes, view

yourself as an observer. Replace insecurity with awe. Repeat the lines: "I am powerful. I am desired. I am in control of my sexuality." Remind yourself that humans have been gathering to have group and kinky sex from the dawn of time. Restraint and judgment are what's new. Carnal desires are not. You are a witch who lives life deliciously and not a muggle who subscribes to sex-negative thinking.

3. Using a purse or pouch, pack your bag. You'll need items for sexual protection such as condoms and other latex barriers and lube (these are often provided at parties, but it can't hurt to bring your own). Toss in crystals for sexual energy such as red jasper, garnet, and smoky or pink quartz. Sprinkle the bag with Venus Powder or spritz it with your favorite perfume. If you're feeling cautious, add crystals such as black tourmaline for protection.

4. Go forth and enjoy your night like the sex witch that you are.

Unleash Your Kinks

You will need: Blue or white candles, a pillow to meditate on, rope or yarn, scissors or safety shears

The best time to cast the spell: The waning moon will help you remove fear and communication blocks.

Sex Witch says

" *Kinks refer to any sexual interest outside of heteronormative vanilla sex. Some people like to be called names during role-playing, and others want to sit on balloons. Some folks want penetration with strap-on dildos and others like pain. As long as your kink involves consenting adults, it should be embraced and enjoyed. What would the Death card say about not fulfilling your*

fantasy? It can understandably take time to both person-
ally embrace your kink and then share them with others.
This spell aims to cut through that fear, so you can be the
kinky sex witch that you are.

The Spell:

1. Light blue candles, or white if that's what you have, on your altar to welcome clarity and communication. Sit on a pillow or meditation mat in front of your altar.

2. Tie your wrist using a basic shibari, or Japanese rope bondage, method:

- Take the center (bight) of your rope. Wrap it around the wrist twice. Make sure to leave room for a couple of fingers to slip in between the rope and the wrist. Cross the bight over the opposite ends of the rope.

  Tuck the bight underneath all the ropes. Remember to reach under and pull the rope instead of pushing it through because it'll retain its lay, or pattern, easier. While we'll use scissors, for potential future shibari purposes, this pattern is easier to slip off and remove while retaining its structure.

- Make a loop with a working end and pull the bight through. Repeat and pull tight on the knot. Place your hands together and wrap the working end around your other wrist as best you can to bind your wrists together. Keep this hand loose enough so you may slip it out to use scissors. It's okay if your hands aren't truly tied together and you can escape. The ropes are symbolic, and you just learned a shibari tie.

3. Sit and meditate on your kink. Let yourself feel the negative emotions associated with it, such as shame and

embarrassment. Let's say that you want to be verbally degraded by your partner. Imagine the ropes as society's restraints. What's wrong with role-playing? Why can't a powerful witch get off on some humiliation? The men of Wall Street do it; why not you? You're smart and magickal enough to understand that the bedroom is a safe space to play and explore and even work out repression.

4. Meditate on what your partner may think. Hint: It will likely turn them on. In the off chance that it makes them uncomfortable, you can always use compromise and baby steps with kinks. And if anyone judges you or is mean about your kink? Introduce them to the spell titled Dump Them on page 186—because you deserve better. Imagine all negative emotions pouring into the rope as you mentally pour out your fears.

5. Flip the script. Meditate on all that can go well if you embrace and share your kink. You can freely enjoy it. You can bond with your partner. You can come your face off.

6. When you feel sexual heat generating to the point it outweighs your fears, grab the shears and snip off the rope. You're free!

7. Keep the candles burning as you please but throw out the rope. Its purpose has been served.

8. Follow through and share your kink with your partner. Try simply saying, "Hey, I've been wanting to try [insert kink here] name-calling during sex. Would you be down to try calling me some dirty names?" Your wish is their command.

Kitchen Witch Massage Oil

You will need: 1 ounce carrier oil, such as coconut or grapeseed oil; essential lavender and vanilla oils; a glass container; rose petals

The best time to cast the spell: Whenever you're ready for home-made touch and pleasure

Sex Witch says

> *Massages are an intimate bonding experience with stress-relieving and physically healing properties. Give your partner a back massage to work out aches and pains or turn it into an erotic massage with a happy ending. Oil can degrade latex, so be mindful if you and your partner use condoms and are intending on having penetrative sex after the massage.*

The Spell:

1. Measure out one ounce of your carrier oil. Coconut smells lovely and is associated with protective properties. If you dislike how coconut oil can thicken, opt for fractionated coconut oil. Another great choice is grapeseed oil, although be aware that it can stain sheets.

2. Add six drops of lavender oil, which promotes relaxation. Add another six drops of vanilla oil, which is associated with Venus and is simultaneously erotic and soothing.

3. Pour your oil into your jar. Add some fresh rose petals for extra romance and beauty. Bless your potion by saying, "May this oil bring pleasure and relaxation to all it touches."

Ease into Anal Sex

You will need: A white or green candle, lubricant, cannabis suppositories, a small butt plug, your partner or a strap-on dildo (there are thinner dildos specifically made for anal sex), condoms if you use them

The best time to cast the spell: Whenever you're ready to have some hot anal sex and want it done right

❝ *The rectum is an erogenous zone loaded with nerve endings. Everyone has a butthole, so anal sex is an inclusive way to fuck. However, unlike the vagina, the anus is not self-lubricating. Without proper preparation, anal sex can be painful and disastrous, leading many to write it off for good. Follow this spell to actually enjoy anal sex. If penetrative anal sex isn't for you, oral anal sex (rimming) or touching are other options to enjoy butt stuff.*

Sex Witch says

The Spell:

1. The name of the game is "relax." Light candles. Dim the lights. Put on ambient music. Curate an environment that speaks to you.

2. Light a green candle for health and protection. Green is the color of earthly matters, which is why we use it for money spells, but it's also grounding. Our root chakra, which grounds us, rules the rectum. We can cause bodily harm to our rectum with irresponsible anal sex, as the lining of the rectum is quite thin. This is where protection comes in. If you don't have a green candle, you can use a white one in its place.

3. Whether it's watching porn or fantasizing, bring yourself to a state of arousal. Our body relaxes and allows for penetration more easily when aroused with heightened blood flow.

4. Wash your hands, and then lube them up. Silicone lube is goopy and lasts a long time, making it a preferred option for anal sex. However, if you're intending on using a silicone sex toy, such as a butt plug or dildo, opt for a water-based variety as silicone degrades silicone. By yourself, or with your partner, insert one finger, and then two. Stick with this form of penetration until it feels comfortable.

5. Always feel free to stimulate your penis or clitoris during anal play. This often makes it feel even better. Just be careful not to use the same hand so you don't transfer bacteria from your rectum into your urethral opening.

6. If you live in a legal state, consider a cannabis suppository. They increase blood flow and reduce pain and inflammation without numbing you out. Check what the suppository is made out of as oils such as coconut oil are not latex-compatible.

7. After you're warmed up, add more lube, and then insert a small butt plug. These sex toys have a flared base to keep them in place. Wear your butt plug for as long as you like, and feel free to engage in other sexual activities while it's in. Some people even enjoy wearing butt plugs in public.

8. Finally, remove the butt plug, add more lube, and practice slow deep breathing as your partner inserts their penis or strap-on dildo into your anus. It may take a few tries to find the right angle and position. Go very slow and use your safeword whenever needed.

Tempted by the Fruit of Another

You will need: A white candle, an apple, a sex toy if you please

The best time to cast the spell: The waning moon will help remove shame and guilt

> **❝** *It's human nature to experience attraction to those other than your partner, even if you're monogamous. Such desires are nothing to feel guilty over. If you're in a committed relationship but lusting after someone forbidden, follow this spell to exorcise your shame so you can have your cake—or in this case, an apple—and eat it too.*

Sex Witch says

The Spell:

1. Place a white candle for clarity and communication on your altar. Light it. Sit in front of your altar with an apple in your hands.

2. Praying to the universe or your deity of choice, say the following incantation: "I accept my desires as natural. I am a sexual being. May I receive clarity and pleasure regarding my desires. May I do no harm."

3. As you sit, meditate upon your desires with the apple in your hand. The apple is a symbol of knowledge and sexual freedom, as demonstrated by Eve in the Garden of Eden. It's associated with many goddesses such as Aphrodite and also with love and fidelity.

4. With the apple in your hands, mentally walk through your options. Do you and your partner have an open relationship or the desire and capacity for one? Is the object of your lust sexually available? If so, see A Tarot Spread to Find Which

Relationship Format is Right for You in chapter 6 after completion of this spell.

5. In most cases, a sexual fantasy is nothing more than a fantasy. Do you actually want to sleep with this person—and all the strings they come with—or do they just make you horny?

6. It's time to have some fun. Now that you've sent the hard questions out to the universe, while holding the apple allow yourself to sexually fantasize about this person. Get as graphic and dirty as possible. Do not hold back. The apple is now fully charged with both your sexual fantasies and your desire to do no harm.

7. Place the apple on your altar next to the white candle. Move to your bed or wherever you masturbate, bringing a sex toy if you need it.

8. Masturbate to the person you're lusting after.

9. After you finish, notice what you feel. Are you still obsessed with this person? Are they a figure worthy of ruining your relationship or simply a fantasy to enjoy?

10. Eat the apple. You are accepting your desires as normal, as well as your good-willed intention of acting upon such fantasies without harm. You have done nothing wrong and are simply a magickal witch and sexual being.

Consecrate Sex Toys

You will need: Your sex toy, sage, Florida Water or holy water (which you can make yourself)

The best time to cast the spell: Venus rules Friday and leads into the weekend. Cast the spell Friday or whenever works for your schedule.

" *Decent sex toys can be pricey but are worth the investment. Ensure your sex toy is made with medical-grade silicone, glass, or metal. Rubber jellies are less expensive but degrade over time, and we don't want it degrading inside our bodies. Anything porous, such as jelly rubber, or what's abbreviated as TBR, is difficult to contain and can harbor bacteria. In addition to magickally cleansing your sex toy, make sure to clean it after each use to avoid UTIs, yeast infections, and bacterial infections. Adult shops sell sex toy cleaner, or you can cleanse most with gentle soap and water. If your sex toy is made of silicone, glass, or steel, and doesn't have a motor (as vibrators do) you can boil it like spaghetti.*

Sex Witch says

The Spell:

1. Hold your sex toy and your sage. Say, "I cleanse this sex toy with the power of earth. It shall bring my body pleasure."

2. Light the sage. Say, "I consecrate this sex toy with the power of fire. It shall unleash my passion."

3. Blow out the fire and run the sex toy through the sage smoke. Say, "I cleanse this sex toy with the power of air. May it bring me knowledge of my true self."

4. Flick a few drops of Florida Water, which can be purchased online or at occult stores, or holy water on your sex toy. You can make holy water by sprinkling salt in a clockwise direction into a bowl of water. Say, "I cleanse and consecrate this water with the power of the witch." As you sprinkle water on your toy, say, "I consecrate this sex toy with the power of water. May it be transformative and emotionally healing."

Hot Sex Incense

You will need: Mortar and pestle, dried rose petals, vanilla bean, myrtle leaves, patchouli leaves, dragon's blood resin, amber resin, a pouch or jar, charcoal tablets, a fireproof surface and tongs

The best time to cast the spell: During the waxing or full moon

Sex Witch says

> *These incenses will be "loose," which means they must be placed on top of a lit charcoal tablet to burn. Remember that it's an honor to be a loose woman or whichever word represents your gender and the vagina cannot actually become loose from too much sex. That is patriarchal muggle talk meant to keep women and other marginalized genders from enjoying sex with as many partners as they please.*
>
> *Hot Sex Incense contains six ingredients, as six is the number corresponding with Venus. After you make it, place some upon a charcoal tablet to use as traditional incense. It can also be left in dishes like potpourri. Burn it during a sexual encounter, while doing love or sex spells, or whenever you wish to invoke the hot sex god(dess) within you.*

The Spell:

1. Using your mortar and pestle, grind the herbs. Roses are a love and beauty staple and associated with Aphrodite. Aphrodite is also often pictured with myrtle leaves in her hair, and this herb is used for love and protection. Vanilla is associated with Venus and self-empowerment. Patchouli conjures lust. Blend them together into a medium-fine powder. Set aside the ground herbs in a different dish.

2. Now we add the resins, which will act as a base. Freeze your resins ahead of time for easier grinding. Dragon's blood is a powerful bloodred ingredient that will enhance any spell. Due to its color, it's associated with passion and amplifies courage. Amber, like the sun it resembles, brings power and strength. Mix the two resins with your mortar and pestle. They will leave residue; which is why we do resins last.

3. Combine your herbs and resins and mix them all together in the mortar and pestle.

4. Store your incense in a pouch or jar. Let it sit for a few weeks, so the mixture may marry. Then, pick up some charcoal tablets and use them as you please. To work with a charcoal tablet, light the tablet and place it on a fireproof surface using tongs. Let it sit for a minute or two until the entire disk is sparkling. Place the loose incense on top.

Psychic Sex Smoke Blend

You will need: A place to meditate, cannabis, dried rose petals, mullein, damiana, rolling papers or a pipe, a lighter

The best time to cast the spell: Whenever you're about to fuck someone's brains out

> 66 *Cannabis and the other herbs, especially when coupled with meditation, elevate our minds to a place where we can deeply connect with our partners and their needs. You may find yourself psychically knowing when a dick needs to be sucked or a pussy needs to be eaten. You'll also confidently ask for and receive what you desire from your partner. P.S.: If all you want to smoke is cannabis, that is a-okay.*

Sex
Witch
says

The Spell:

1. Prepare yourself a cozy meditation space before a date or a lover comes over.

2. Create your psychic smoke blend. If you're prone to anxiety during sex, opt for an indica or cannabis strain high in CBD. If you're feeling lethargic, go for an energizing sativa or strain high in THC. Dried rose petals connect you to your heart chakra and offer a romantic aphrodisiac. Mullein is often used as a base in smoking blends and can offer pain relief. It's also a slight sedative. Damiana is an ancient aphrodisiac with a smooth and spicy taste. Combine the herbs in a manner that fits your needs.

3. Roll a joint, pack a bowl or bong, or use whatever is your preferred smoking method.

4. Sitting in your comfy meditation spot, take a few hits of your magickal smoke blend.

5. Close your eyes and begin meditating. As you do, imagine a bright ruby sparkling where your heart is. Notice your heart beating. As the blood pumps through your body and through your genitals and every erogenous zone, visualize the majestic red spreading throughout your body.

6. Imagine your partner. Visualize their body; picture making love to them. Where do you want to touch? What do you want to do to them? What do you want them to do to you?

7. When you're ready, come out of the meditation. Use your smoke blend as you please, and feel free to share it with your partner. Maintain your heightened state of mind to be completely in the moment during sex and unburdened by insecurities.

Watch Sexual Fantasies Come Alive

You will need: Fresh roses, the Death card from a tarot deck, a saucepan with a lid, water, a cheesecloth or other strainer

The best time to cast the spell: Use the waxing moon to encourage your sexual fantasies to blossom.

> ❝ *Kinky fantasies are extremely common. For instance, more than half of women (52.1 percent) and nearly half of men (46.2 percent) fantasize about being tied up during sex. Online kink forums host groups for everything from balloon fetishes to fem domme. However, most of us were not taught to embrace our kinks but to seek out a heteronormative relationship that involves a lot of missionary sex with the purpose of procreating. Whether you just want to fuck to come rather than conceive or are ready to bring a fantasy to life, this spell aims to walk you through that. Witches understand that sex is meant to be good messy fun.*

Sex Witch says

The Spell:

1. Sit in a meditative pose with your tarot deck and roses by your side.

2. Marvel at your roses. White and red roses work great, but any color that speaks to you will do. Smell them, touch their soft petals, carefully run your fingers over their thorns. Charge one rose by holding it and thinking about your sexual fantasy.

3. Admire the Death card. In the Rider-Waite tarot deck, we see Death riding on a white horse, carrying a flag adorned with a white rose. The Death card rarely represents a physical death, but a rebirth. It is often a sign of new beginnings. For that to happen, we must let old ways of thinking (or fucking) die. In

astrology, the Death card corresponds to Scorpio, which is the sign of death and rebirth. Imagine Death taking away all your thoughts and fears holding you back from living your sexual truth.

4. The rose represents your desires and must be reborn. Hang the rose in a cool dark place. It will take two to three weeks to dry fully.

5. Once your rose is dried, crumble the petals and place ¼ cup into a saucepan. Add 1½ cups of water.

6. Cover and bring to a boil.

7. Reduce the temperature and bring to a simmer. Let the rose water simmer for seven minutes or until the color in the petals fades.

8. Let the water cool. When it's room temperature, transfer into a bottle.

9. Rose water can be used as a perfume, room spray, or as part of your skin routine. Your rose water demonstrates your internal rebirth surrounding your sexual fantasies. Spray the rose water to clear the air whenever you feel bad about your-self or to bless a room before hot sex is going to happen.

Summon a Threesome

You will need: Two red candles, one white candle, Come to Me Oil

The best time to cast the spell: The new moon is a wonderful time for sex and love spells and represents new beginnings and journeys—which adding a third to your relationship absolutely is.

" *Threesomes can be hot AF, but they can also end disastrously. The name of the game is communication. If you're in a committed relationship, you must discuss boundaries with your partner, such as which sex acts are okay and which are off limits. You must also discuss STI testing and safer sex practices with both your partner and your third. Often couples turn to dating apps, but it can be helpful to use apps and websites created specifically for hookups so you don't waste people's time who are looking for a serious partner. Do you want a stranger or someone you know? You also need to answer that question. If you want a no-strings-attached threesome and have the budget, often hiring a sex worker is your best bet.*

Sex Witch says

While we most commonly hear about the FFM (female, female, male) threesome, don't let that bullshit stop you for going after the MMF (male, male, female) threesome of your fantasies. Also, threesomes can be queer and done with any gender or orientation. I once watched a gay man wear a strap-on and have a threesome with two lesbians at the Chelsea Hotel on a full moon—now that was magickal.

The Spell:

1. Talk to your partner to decide what you're looking for. Who is your ideal threesome candidate? How do you want to find them? Do you prefer an acquaintance or a stranger?

2. In the shape of a triangle, set up two red candles and one white candle. The red candles represent you and your partner, and the white candle represents the opportunity of the third.

3. Anoint the white candle with Come to Me Oil. If you're feeling bold, use the sexual fluids of you and your partner to anoint the candle.

4. Light the red candle to the right. Say, "I shall enjoy a threesome with no detriment to my relationship."

5. Light the red candle to the left. Say, "My partner [or use name] shall enjoy a threesome with no detriment to our relationship."

6. Light the white candle. Say, "Our third shall enjoy a threesome with no detriment to our relationship. So, mote it be."

7. When the candles finish burning, the spell is complete.

Practice Sex Magick with a Partner

You will need: You and your partner

The best time to cast the spell: Sex magick is best for manifestation, rather than banishing work, so utilize the waxing or full moon.

Sex Witch says

> *Sex magick is often practiced alone as masturbation for minimal interference. However, it can be done with a partner so long as they're on board. It's okay if they don't identify as a witch, but they need to take the goal seriously. If someone mocks sex magick, do not involve them. And if someone is an asshole to you about it, dump them!*

The Spell:

1. Meet with your partner. Decide upon a shared desire, such as obtaining more money or landing a job one of you is after.

2. Fuck. You want to have fun, so please enjoy. Keep your goal in mind and visualize sexual energy going toward that goal.

3. When one or both of you orgasm, bring your mind back to your goal. Use your visualization skills to see yourself as your desires become reality. See your combined sexual energy feeding that goal.

Survive a Dry Spell

You will need: A pen and paper, water, a lighter, chamomile tea bags, a bathtub, lavender essential oil, sea salt

The best time to cast the spell: Use the waning moon to wash off negative thoughts and assumptions.

> ❝ As horny humans who crave companionship, we all know dry spells can suck. Especially after a rough breakup, it's easy to let your mind spiral. You may feel convinced that you're unfuckable or will never love again. This is so far from the truth. You must change your mindset and embrace this period as a time in which you are free to do whatever—and whoever—you want. Your last breakup may have been painful, but it was a necessary step in your journey. Trust in the universe that a healthier love awaits.

Sex Witch says

The Spell:

1. Write down all your fears on a piece of paper. If you fear that your last breakup was a mistake, write that down. If you fear no one will ever want to have sex with you, write that down. If you feel you're too this or too that to ever find love, write that down. Let it out.

2. On another piece of paper, begin to reverse your statements. For instance, if you wrote that you're "too crazy for a relationship," rewrite that as "my next relationship will be with someone interesting enough to understand me." If you wrote "No one wants to fuck me," rewrite that as "I look forward to meeting my next sexual partner." If you wrote, "I'm alone," rewrite that as "I am free."

3. Begin to boil enough water for a pot of tea.

4. As the water is boiling, light your first list of fears over the sink. Let it burn.

5. When the water is ready, add chamomile tea bags to make chamomile tea.

6. As the tea steeps, run a bath. Place your lavender oil and list of positive statements near the bath.

7. Toss a handful of cleansing and purifying sea salts into the running bathwater.

8. Pour yourself a cup of tea to drink, and then add the rest of the chamomile tea into your bathwater. Chamomile is soothing to the body and associated magickally with strength in adversity and manifesting love.

9. Add ten drops of lavender essential oil to the bath. The number ten refers to the end of a cycle. For instance, the image on the 10 of Swords in the tarot is at first glance one of despair. However, closer study reveals that this card refers to the phrase "It's always darkest before dawn." Lavender, like chamomile, is soothing and relaxing. Now is the time to shed your fears, know that love and sex await, and be strong, free, and learn from previous romantic missteps.

10. Lower your body into the tub. Let the salt soak out all those self-deprecating thoughts and the chamomile and lavender soothe you. Sip on your tea and chill out as you meditate on your list of positive statements. Say them out loud as you enjoy your bath.

11. Get out of the bath and get to work on having some fun. Let the demons that want you to feel badly about yourself swirl away down the drain with the bathwater.

Have Makeup Sex

You will need: Two red candles, a love oil or bodily fluids or hair from you and your partner if possible, one green candle

The best time to cast the spell: The waning moon will help you remove hurt, but honestly, cast this spell whenever you need to. Love is not always patient and sometimes requires immediate attention.

> **❝** *It is important to be aware and clear on your boundaries. For instance, if someone speaks to you in an abusive manner, dump them. However, it's important to consider that the age of swiping makes it easy to throw out relationships we don't actually wish to end. Humans mess up. Sometimes it's cheating and sometimes it's blurting out the wrong thing. Except for cases where abuse is involved, the only one who can decide if forgiveness is in order is you. If you want to forgive and make up, have some magick sex.*

Sex Witch says

The Spell:

1. After cleansing, hold a red candle in your hand. This candle represents your partner. Meditate on what you fought

over and the hurt. Talk to the candle. Tell it how much it hurt you. Then tell it that you forgive it.

2. Coat the red candle in love oil or, if available, your partner's seminal or vaginal fluid. Placing their hair on the candle also works. Put it on the altar to the right.

3. Hold the second red candle in your hand. This represents you. Meditate on the decision of forgiveness. Anoint this candle as well in love oil or your own seminal or vaginal fluid. Add your hair on the candle if desired. Menstrual blood is also extremely potent. Place it on the altar to the left.

4. Hold the green candle, which represents healing and the energetic child of your relationship. Place it at the top of the altar in between the two candles. No, the red and green are not for Christmas, you perv. They are for passion and health.

5. Say out loud, "With the power of love, I forgive you for your actions. With the power of mercy, I understand and let go. With the power of passion, we courageously move forward."

6. Light the candles. Understand that as they burn away, so does any lingering resentments and, by casting the spell, you promise to move forward with your partner.

7. Find your partner and ensure they understand everything you told the candles.

8. Have hot makeup sex as the candles burn.

Slut It Up

You will need: Lingerie, music, a spell bag, seven apple seeds, a dash of damiana, a dash of sugar, a slice of ginger, black tourmaline, safer sex latex barrier and lube

The best time to cast the spell: The waxing moon will help you wax on with more partners, and the full moon brings a full sex life.

> 66 *It is not always the time for committed relationships. Sometimes it is time to be a slut—which is a compliment in this book—and have lots of hot sex with as many people as you want. Such periods of freedom are an opportunity to discover niche sexual interests such as new kinks or sex parties. You'll be glad you have such stories to tell your grandchildren or kittens.*

Sex Witch says

The Spell:

1. When you're alone and able to be completely free, put on an outfit of lingerie that makes you feel ultrahot. Do you like dancing naked? Even better.

2. Put on your favorite slut anthem. We all have one!

3. Dance with complete freedom. Be disgusting. Hold nothing back and use your body to convey what a sex god(dess) you are.

4. When you're sweaty and finished dancing, grab your spell bag. A spell bag can be quickly sewn or purchased online. They are also called charm bags and gris-gris bags in the Voodoo tradition. They are worn around your neck and safely tucked away while showering.

5. Place seven apple seeds in the spell bag. Apple represents the snake of seduction, which is exactly what we want. Eat the rest of the apple if you like.

6. Add a dash of damiana, an herb hailed for its aphrodisiac properties, to the bag.

7. Throw in a dash of sugar to attract lovers with sweetness.

8. Insert a slice of ginger. Ginger attracts adventure and confidence and is used in seduction and love spells.

9. Add a small chunk of black tourmaline for protection.

10. Crystals cannot protect you from STIs. You must act like a modern slut. Stock up on latex barriers such as condoms or dental dams. Store them somewhere room temperature away from sunlight and sharp objects. It's okay to place them in your purse or pocket for a night out, but they need a safer permanent storage space.

11. Lube is important even if you have a vagina. A dry condom will rip. It's time to normalize lube use. As a witch, it's your duty to protect yourself and be sexually progressive.

12. Go forth and be slutty. Often, when a spell bag breaks or falls off, it means the spell is complete. While you don't have to stop sleeping with whoever you like when the spell bag breaks, take it as a sign to check in with yourself.

Aftercare Ointment

You will need: 10 grams dried ground cannabis, parchment paper, a baking sheet, an oven and stove, 2½ cups coconut oil, a saucepan, eucalyptus essential oil, 1 cup aloe vera, 1 teaspoon vitamin E oil, 2 tablespoons cocoa butter, cheesecloth, a jar

The best time to cast the spell: Cast this spell whenever you have time for an epic kitchen witch session.

66 *Witches understand that herbs hold many properties. Even if you're not a cannabis consumer, you can
benefit from the nonpsychoactive, anti-inflammatory,
and pain-relieving properties of the plant as part of this
all-natural and vegan aftercare ointment. There is evidence that witches used cannabis topicals for healing in
ancient times.*

*What is aftercare? It's a fancy name used by kink-
sters for taking care of one another after sex. That
includes verbally checking in but can also mean treat-
ing bruises if you engaged in impact play or use of
objects against the skin such as whips, paddles, or the
hand for spanking. Apply this magickal ointment to
treat bruises and other common sex injuries.*

Sex Witch says

The Spell:

1. First, you need to decarboxylate your cannabis, which
is the magickal practice of turning buds into psychoactive
herbs. It's why you can't get high by just chewing on weed.
To do this, set your oven to 230 degrees Fahrenheit. Spread
parchment paper over a baking tray. Sprinkle your ground
cannabis evenly over the parchment paper. Stick it in the
oven and bake for forty-five minutes.

2. Place your coconut oil in a saucepan and stir on low. Coconut oil is moisturizing and reduces inflammation like cannabis. Witches historically use it for healing and beauty. Slowly
mix in the decarboxylated cannabis and stir the two together
for twenty minutes.

3. Maintaining a very low heat so the cannabis doesn't burn,
add ten drops of eucalyptus oil. Like cannabis, eucalyptus
treats bruising and is nourishing to the skin. It's known in
witchcraft for protection and healing.

4. Stir in one cup of aloe vera, which heals, soothes, and nourishes skin as stated in both medical and magickal records.

5. Add one teaspoon of vitamin E oil for maximum skin health, and two tablespoons of cocoa butter. In addition to moisturizing, cocoa butter is said to soak through the skin for stress relief.

6. Remove the mixture from heat and strain through cheesecloth into a jar.

7. Speaking into your ointment, say, "May true love reign, and this ointment wane, hot sex pain and kinky sprains." Seal the lid and look forward to its use.

6. Magick for love

Love is both a divine experience and a human one that needs care and nurturing. It's not just about sex, kids; sometimes, you can have sex and be in love at the same time! While spark is essential for an exciting relationship, love does not merely live forever on its own. Shit happens. You move in together and learn which foods make the other one fart. We must nurture our relationships, address issues as they arise, and honor a commitment. And that's after you settle into a relationship! Think of all the massaging new love needs so that you don't blow it up to avoid the whole thing. The following love spells aim to maintain a healthy and loving relationship through spellwork and intention.

Tame Jealousy

You will need: One blue candle, a pen and notebook

The best time to cast the spell: The waning moon

> ❝ *Blue is the color of tranquility in addition to communication and clarity. Hold a blue candle to charge it with all of the fear, suspicion, trauma, and insecurities forming your jealousy. Then burn the candle while following this ritual to identify why you are jealous and what communication needs to happen to uncover if you have reason. Manifest strength and clarity to communicate with your partner and banish jealousy as the blue candle burns away.*

Sex Witch says

The Spell:

1. We all feel jealous regardless of if we're monogamous or polyamorous. It's not a bad emotion, and you're not wrong to feel it. However, it is an emotion that can disrupt a relationship. So let's get ahead of it.

2. Sit down with all those jealous thoughts. Grab your blue candle. We're going to go to the bad place. Think every last petty, mean, angry, scared, and insecure thought that you have had. Imagine all that dark, slimy energy going out of your body and mind and into the candle.

3. Place the candle on your altar and let it burn.

4. While the candle is burning, write down what you're jealous about. Is it another person? Are you jealous about their appearance, their success, or what they can offer your partner? Obviously every situation is different, but once we identify what we're jealous of, it's easier to understand why. An insecurity is usually underneath the jealousy. Whatever is making you jealous may bring out negative thoughts on how you look, what you do for a living, where you're from, etc.

5. Now consider all that you have that likely makes others jealous. Think about what makes you attractive, happy, and successful in your own right. Remind yourself that everyone's paths are different and there isn't one way to go about the world. Someone else may threaten you, but that doesn't mean they're better than you.

6. From a calmer perspective, have an honest conversation with your partner. Communication is everything. Check in to be honest about what's going on and to see what they think. Is there any reason to worry? If not, hell yeah! If there is, be adults and come up with a solution.

7. When the candle is finished burning away all of your insecurities infused into it, the spell is complete.

A Tarot Spread to Find Which Relationship Format Is Right for You

You will need: A tarot deck, a pen and paper

The best time to cast the spell: Whenever you are seeking clarity

> 66 *Are you considering an open relationship? It's not as simple as monogamy versus polyamory. The two exist on a spectrum, and there are as many ways to be in love as there are people. You must know if you're more uncomfortable with emotional intimacy with others or sexual intimacy, among other questions. Use the tarot while following this question guide on relationship formats to help you discover which relationship format is best in your case.*

Sex Witch says

The Spell:

1. Polyamory is so trendy it almost feels boring to be monogamous! However, polyamory is not for everyone, and neither is monogamy. There is no right way to love. The only irresponsible relationship format is one that denies your truth. To begin, how are you with love and emotions? Polyamory translates to "many loves"; can you see yourself with not only more than one sexual partner, but loving more than one person? How do you feel about your partner loving other people? Pull a card.

2. You must also consider your relationship to sex. Do you feel safer with one sexual partner, or do you feel trapped by the idea of only having sex with one person? Do you want the freedom to explore? What about group sex, play parties, and other activities in which sex with others *and* your partner is open to you? How do you feel about your partner sleeping with other people? Scared? Angry? Turned on? Pull a card.

3. Open relationships can be emotionally exclusive and sexually open; however, even when we draw clear boundaries, we don't always abide by them. Can you have just sex with others, or do you tend to fall in love easily? Can you handle the messiness inherent in all relationships, but especially open ones? Pull a card.

4. Gaze upon your spread. Does each card teach you something? Do they tell you what you already know or open up your eyes to new perspectives? Does the third card help make sense out of the first two?

5. Write down some notes and thoughts about what you're feeling. For some people, a relationship format such as polyamory feels like an inherent part of their sexuality, like an orientation. For others, it ebbs and flows depending on their situation or the person or people they're dating. How you feel today may be how you feel tomorrow, or you could feel entirely different then. The only action required of you is to be honest with yourself about your needs and communicate them to your partner(s).

Forgive Someone You Love

You will need: A pen and paper, a bathtub, bath salts, a bouquet of white flowers

The best time to cast the spell: The new moon

> ❝ When you are ready to let go of old wounds once and for all, take a ritual bath, and then use white flowers to absorb the remaining negative energy. Toss them in a body of water to be done with the resentment. Stay true to your work and word and move forward with your relationship to the future joy that awaits.

Sex Witch says

The Spell:

1. We all get mad. We all definitely get mad at the people we fuck. Is it something in our genes—who knows? Yes, they fuck up and are idiots. But if we can step back from the urgency of our hearts and genitals and the thin line between hate and love, happiness awaits. If the crime committed is forgivable, forgive.

2. First, let's get that hate out. Write down everything that you're mad about. Do not hold back. No one will see this letter.

3. As you write, run a hot bath. Pour bath salts into the running water. Salts purify and remove toxins—like all that hate in you. Any bath salts work. Use your favorite lavender-scented ones or whatever floats your boat; there are tons available from both beauty and occult stores.

4. Set the bouquet of white flowers next to the bath.

5. Soak in the bath until the water becomes cool. Visualize your anger drawing out of you like poison.

6. Open the drain and get out of the bathtub. Watch the water and all your anger swirl down the drain.

7. Let's be real. You're not 100 percent done being mad yet. Rip up your letter and put the pieces in a baggie or something that you can carry.

8. Brush the white bouquet of flowers over your naked body. Use the white flowers, a symbol of fresh stars, to dust off lingering anger and open your heart for forgiveness.

9. Get dressed and go out and scatter the pieces of paper and white flowers at a crossroads.

10. Live up to your spell. Forgiveness is a choice. Let what happened go, learn, and move forward.

A Spell for Clear Communication

You will need: A pen and paper, a goblet, water, citrine

The best time to perform this spell: The full moon

Sex Witch says

> *Before we can communicate our needs, we must understand them. This multipurpose spell uses journaling to communicate in the most efficient way possible. Then, with the aid of magickally charged water and an amulet for courage, you share your needs with your partner. While we can magickally encourage our partner to reciprocate, ultimately it is on each of us to keep our side of the street clean, and this spell addresses options if healthy communication is one-way.*

The Spell:

1. Relationships can be frustrating. Our partner may play hot and cold, and we may take months to define the relationship.

Regardless of the circumstances, the way out of confusion is through communication. Journaling is a therapeutic tool that helps us identify what we want and become grounded enough to communicate it to others. Write out how you're feeling and what you want to express. Fold up the piece of paper.

2. Fill a goblet or glass with filtered water on the next full moon. Place it on top of the folded piece of paper on a windowsill or somewhere exposed to moonlight. You will need a piece of citrine, which is a readily available crystal. It's often associated with career prosperity, because it's a stone of confidence and abundance. The stone helps you step into boldness and clarity and realize your worth. Place the citrine in the goblet.

3. Let the goblet sit overnight under the full moon so it becomes charged with power.

4. The next morning, gently remove the citrine from the glass. Drink the water. You are drinking in your intentions and the confidence to communicate them to the subject of your letter. Feel the power course through you.

5. With calm boldness and integrity, ask to hang out with your love interest, and communicate your needs and questions with grace.

Bless an Intercultural Relationship

You will need: A 6-by-6-inch piece of white fabric, moonstone, two rose petals, two apple seeds, black tourmaline, snippets of your and your love's hair, a piece of red ribbon, sage

The best time to cast the spell: Friday

"While intercultural and interracial couples have always faced discrimination, a world in which certain religions and countries are banned from entering this one isn't helping matters. Intercultural relationships are difficult but can be the most rewarding. Use this protective spell to keep away awful outside influences.

The Spell:

1. Lay out the white piece of fabric. While white people are responsible for most of the world's problems and certainly not representative of protection in real life, the actual color white acts as a divine safeguard. Let's wrap you two beautiful love birds up in some of that.

2. Place the moonstone in the middle of the fabric. Moonstone is used to increase empathy. Most of us, especially white folks, can always stand to apply more empathy to others.

3. Place two rose petals representing romance and you and your partner in the middle of the fabric.

4. Add two apple seeds for protection.

5. Place a chunk of black tourmaline for super-duper protection.

6. Optionally, sprinkle this with snippets of your and your partner's hair to amplify the potency of the spell.

7. Using a red ribbon to symbolize love, tie up the fabric into a sack. This represents your sacred protected love.

8. Light sage and hold it underneath the pouch to cleanse and remove any unwanted clinging energies.

9. Keep the bag somewhere safe, such as in your underwear drawer or on your altar. Understand that unfortunately,

spells are not enough to combat the evils of the world unless they are done with follow-through. Check in with your partner. Educate yourself on their culture. Be ready to mess up. Be ready to own up to mistakes. Be ready to forgive. Be brave enough to have an ongoing conversation.

Survive Long Distance

You will need: A view of the moon, a physical or electronic calendar, a black candle, means to contact your lover, flowers

The best time to cast the spell: During a period of separation between you and your loved one

> 66 *Maintain a calendar and a love altar guided by the light of the moon to ensure you tend to your long-distance relationship as you tend to your altar. Use the calendar to curate loving contact with your partner from flower deliveries to handwritten poems. As the moon cycles, so will your relationship, reminding you that physical separation is not forever.*

Sex Witch says

The Spell:

1. There are cycles in all areas of our life: money, romance, and love. Sometimes a couple experiences a brief or prolonged physical separation due to work, family, or one partner's decision to attend Burning Man. During this separation, use the moon, the ultimate shape-shifter, to remind you that nothing is temporary. Ensure that you have a view of the moon. Gaze upon it and remember that everyone can see it—including your love—regardless of how far apart you are. Set up a calendar, physically or online, which tracks the moon phases as well as your and your partner's schedule.

2. During the waning phase the moon appears to get smaller. This is a powerful time to remove hexes and negative thoughts and influences. Burn a black candle to banish any unwanted energies picked up during your time apart.

3. During the new moon phase the sky is at its darkest. This is a time of fresh starts and new beginnings. It's the perfect time to set intentions for yourself and your relationship. Send your love some flowers.

4. During the first quarter of the lunar cycle, the moon is in its waxing phase. It appears to grow. Use this phase to remind yourself that growth comes from all experiences, including difficult ones—especially difficult ones. Send your partner a care package.

5. Finally, the full moon is a lunar orgasm, a culmination. This powerful time also brings out our animal instincts. Send your lover sexts and practice sex magick.

Meet the Parents

You will need: Lavender essential oil, an outfit and makeup that make you happy and confident

The best time to cast the spell: When you hear the words: "My mom is in town."

Sex Witch says

66 *Too often people try to make themselves into something they aren't to impress a partner's parents. This ritual uses self-love and glamour magick techniques so that when you meet the parents, you feel confident in yourself and aware that they are someone their child is lucky to receive love from.*

The Spell:

1. So it's time to meet the parents. Check in with yourself. How are you feeling? As someone whose work revolves around sex and the occult, I typically feel panic, especially if parents are religious. Regardless of your profession, meeting the old folks who spawned the person you're going down on is stressful. Let's begin with a calming meditation.

2. Sit down with your lavender essential oil. Place a few drops under your nose. Begin the fourfold breath. Inhale for four counts, hold for four counts, exhale for four counts, hold for four counts. Let the lavender calm you.

3. With each exhale, name an accomplishment or something awesome about yourself.

4. Continue with this breath pattern until you settle upon a mantra, such as "I am the shit." Return to this mantra when you're getting ready or when you're with the actual parents.

5. Deliberately get dressed and do your makeup for this big encounter.

Level Up Love

You will need: Two white candles and one red candle, an object that is sacred to your relationship

The best time to cast the spell: The waxing moon

> ❝ *This spell uses three candles: one for you, one for your partner, and one to represent the relationship or combined energies. Complete with a guided reflection to ensure the time is right, use this spell when you want to take your relationship to the next level—becoming "official," moving in together, etc.*

Sex Witch says

The Spell:

1. Sit down somewhere quiet and comfortable. Keep your three candles in front of you.

2. Pick up a white candle. This represents you. What do you love about yourself? Close your eyes, hold the candle, and infuse it with self-love. Gas yourself up. Go hard. Compliment yourself so much it feels over the top.

3. Pick up the other white candle. This is your partner. What do you love about them? Think about everything from sexual pleasure to personality traits; do not hold back!

4. Pick up the third red candle. As you do, think about what you create together. When two people are in a relationship, a third being is created. What is yours like? How do you learn from one another? How do you turn each other on? How do you grow from your differences and challenges?

5. Place the red candle at the top of your altar and the two white candles below to form a triangle. In the middle of the triangle, place your sacred object that reminds you of the relationship.

6. Light the candles. When they are finished burning, the spell is complete.

Make a Honey Jar

You will need: A piece of paper and a pen, a small glass jar (a 4-ounce mason jar works perfectly), honey, glitter, rose petals, red wine

The best time to cast the spell: On a Friday, which is the day ruled by Venus

> ❝ *A honey jar uses the sacred sticky power of honey combined with herbs for love—and pieces of each other's hair, if possible—to sweeten and preserve a relationship. Honey jars are meant to be kept on a shelf or altar like a snow globe, as a keepsake and not a quick spell. They last a long time and can be a pain to throw out and away—so be careful what you wish for!*

Sex Witch says

The Spell:

1. On a piece of paper, write an intention letter of what you wish to manifest in your love life. Boil it down into one sentence, and then translate your desire into a sigil. Draw the sigil on another piece of paper and fold it up small enough to place in the bottom of your empty jar.

2. Taste your honey with your finger to make sure it's not poisoned! We witches must act as poison testers for goddesses sometimes. Use enough to fill up the jar about ²/₃ of the way.

3. Sprinkle as much glitter as you want on top of the honey.

4. Do the same with dried rose petals.

5. Pour red wine to fill the remainder of the jar.

6. Close the lid tightly and shake it up! Place it somewhere safe and out of harm's reach.

7. Should you ever wish to get rid of the spell, scrub out the honey jar wearing gloves and dispose of the container.

Love Necromancy: Bring Relationships Back to Life

You will need: Fresh ginger, red felt, a black Sharpie, scissors, needle and thread, cotton balls, salt, rosemary, hair or other remnants of you and your partner (optional), a red candle, red ribbon

The best time to cast the spell: The new moon

> *Invoke this spell, which uses dolls, when a relationship is hurt by negative outside forces and in desperate need of repair. It will not work in any desirable manner if only one party is interested.*

The Spell:

1. Before you begin, eat a small sliver of sliced fresh ginger. This adds heat into your workings.

2. Stack two pieces of red felt on top of one another. Draw two human shapes. Make them thick and not too narrow so they're easier to sew. Draw on any defining characteristics using a Sharpie, as well as the name and zodiac symbol of you and your partner.

3. Cut out the two human shapes through the two pieces of felt so you have four total.

4. Stitch two sides up together into two dolls leaving the heads open.

5. Fill them up gently with cotton balls. Add a pinch of salt and a pinch of rosemary to each. Add a slice of ginger. Finally, if you are using hair or other bodily identifications, add those. Sew up the heads of the dolls.

6. On your altar or wherever you're working, create a circle of salt wide enough to contain both dolls. Place a red candle at the top of the circle and light it.

7. Place the dolls on top of one another and wrap them up with red ribbon until they are comfortably attached.

8. Run the feet of each doll lightly over the candle, far enough away so they don't catch fire. Chant "Ribbons entwine, your heart to mine, our love aligns with the protection of the divine."

9. Place the two dolls below the candle in the middle of the salt circle. Practicing fire safety and snuffing the candle out when you leave your home, keep the dolls here until the candle is finished burning.

10. Have a conversation with your partner. What happened? Was it work, or family, or attraction to another that caused a rift? Can you repair it? Do you need time apart, or lots of sex, or to consider opening up your relationship? As the spell is working, you must make a concerted adult effort to communicate with your partner and address how to improve and protect the relationship.

11. When the candle is done burning, discard the dolls. It's okay to just throw them out. The magick is done: they are only felt and craft supplies now.

Candle for Compassion

You will need: A paper and pen, sage, a pink pullout candle, a candle-carving tool, honey, white or pink flowers, incense that reminds you of your partner, a coaster or small plate, love oil, newspaper

The best time to cast the spell: Whenever you need to feel connected to your partner

> 66 *Sometimes all we need to pull a relationship out of a rut is a little compassion for our partner. Carve and light this candle when you realize that your anger or resentment toward your partner is out of line and you need help entering an empathetic and compassionate mind space. Then let them know how much they mean to you.*

Sex Witch says

The Spell:

1. Is your partner annoying you? Perhaps they are extrawhiny or less available than usual due to work, stress, or just some shit that they're dealing with. External factors affect relationships, but when we're really into someone, it's worth it to trudge through a rough patch. Don't you want them to do the same thing for you? Sit down with your pen and paper and meditate on what your partner is going through. Try to get into their mindset and out of your own. In what ways can you empathize with them? Have you perhaps been a bit selfish? Note your realizations using a pen and paper.

2. Boil your intentions and realizations down to one sentence. It can be as simple as "I care about [insert partner's name]." Repeat this mantra in your head as you perform the spell.

3. Using the sigil-making instructions on page 69, turn that sentence into a sigil to carve into the candle.

4. Sage the candle and your other tools. Remove the pink candle from its case. While red is the color of passion, pink is a softer love. It's a caring, empathetic, compassionate love, which is exactly what's needed here.

5. Squirt honey into the base of the glass container. Don't forget to taste it first to make sure it's not poisoned!

6. On top of the honey, sprinkle some white and pink flower petals. For this spell, they can be either fresh or dried.

7. Light your love incense and fill up the glass container. Place the plate or coaster on top to hold in the smoke. Draw the pink candle through the incense as well.

8. On top of the newspaper, begin to carve your sigil into the candle. You can also add your partner's name and zodiac sign.

9. Cover it in love oil.

10. Remove the lid and plop the candle into its glass case. Place it on your altar and light it up.

11. Talk to your partner. Let them know that you're here for them and apologize if you've been a dick. Even better? Buy them flowers!

Move Past the Three-Month Mark

You will need: The stamina to deal with sexual frustration

The best time to cast the spell: The full or waxing moon

> ❝ *Around three months is usually the time when the new relationship endorphins subside and a romance fizzles out or gets more serious. Use sex magick with your partner to continue the hot sex with the mutual desire for something long term. Yes, some witches say that performing sex magick with a partner without their knowledge is unethical, but you know what? All's fair in love and war.*

Sex Witch says

The Spell:

1. So you're in a new relationship and you want to make sure it turns into a long-term one. Let's cast some sex magick to take care of that, shall we?

2. Do not masturbate or have an orgasm for one week. One week! Can you do it? Your suffering is your sacrifice to the love gods.

3. During this time, meditate daily. I've said this before—witches must master the power of visualization. Daily meditation is a great way to sharpen visualization and psychic abilities. What do you want? Is it an image of you happily enjoying dinner together? Fucking? Getting married? Going on vacation? Pick your happy future and visualize it in all its details.

4. After the week of sacrificial orgasm denial has concluded, get ready to come your face off. If you have trouble orgasming, don't worry, your sacred sexual energy is more than enough.

5. Make love to your partner. Be wholly present. The week without orgasm rebuilt sexual tension, which unfortunately, often takes a bit of a nosedive after the early days of the relationship.

6. When you come, pull up your visualization. See it clear as day.

7. Ta-da! Return to fucking your partner.

Moving in Together House Blessing

You will need: A broom, sage, white flowers, a blue candle, clearance or uncrossing incense, candle-carving supplies, newspaper, love oil

The best time to cast the spell: As soon as you move into a new home or apartment. You can even cast this spell for Airbnbs or at other short-term vacation homes.

Sex Witch says

Moving in together is a big deal. Congrats! It's not easy. You will hear the sound of your partner's awful guilty pleasure TV show and bicker about old food in the fridge. However, you also get to wake up next to one another every day and begin a life together.

You can create a love nest that's all your own. However, we must get rid of any residue left behind by the previous residents. You don't want their problems haunting you!

The Spell:

1. Get out your broom, witch. The first thing you need to do is sweep away all the literal dirt and dust left behind. Do you find cleaning degrading, and not in a hot way? Get your partner to do it.

2. Sage the entire home starting in a clockwise circle. Make sure to get in all the corners.

3. Place bouquets of white flowers around the home. They don't have to be expensive. White flowers symbolize new beginnings and peace. Plus, they make your home look so pretty!

4. Carve a blue (for tranquility) home blessing candle. Use a pullout candle if you can. Remove the candle from its glass shell and sage inside the glass and around the candle. Light clearance or uncrossing incense to help exterminate any lingering nasties in the house.

5. Carve an image of a home into the blue candle. It can be a rudimentary drawing, of course. It's the thought that counts.

6. Carve you and your partner's names and zodiac symbols into the candle.

7. Anoint the candle with love oil to encourage the love between you and your partner.

8. Set the candle somewhere pretty and light it up.

9. Go fuck to consecrate the new space.

Have It All: Balancing Ambition and Love

You will need: A tarot deck, an altar, your computer

The best time to cast the spell: Anytime

Sex Witch says

> ❝ It is hard to go after your dreams—whether that's run a business or manage a home—and have time for your relationship. And then there's your friends, the need for alone time, going to the gym, etc. Plus, you might have cats. Shared Google calendars are not just for poly people—although they are highly useful! Striving to find a work-life balance is not a cliché; it's real shit. Cast this spell to magickally and muggley balance ambition and romantic lives.

The Spell:

1. Sit comfortably with your tarot deck. Take out the Hermit card, representative of Virgo. Gaze upon him and the wisdom he has. He understands that he can't do his job if he doesn't retreat. He trusts that those around him understand that his nature requires alone time, and that there's nothing selfish about it. Look into the Hermit card. What else do you see? Place him to the left on your altar.

2. Take out the Lovers card, representative of Gemini. Look at the two figures, often depicted naked, vulnerable, and equal. This is a card of abundance, joy, and the wealth that love produces. An angel blesses them from above; the ground supports them from below. Their joy and love and sexual energy are sacred. Place him to the right on your altar.

3. Finally, take out the Justice card, representative of Virgo. Justice holds the scales of balance. Justice knows when to give and when to take. It balances the facets of existence in

a way that maintains order while encouraging bliss. Place Justice above the Hermit and the Lovers, touching both cards. Meditate in front of the spread and leave it out for seven days.

4. Once you're calm, do something truly far-out. Have a conversation with your partner about your schedules. Where is contact lacking? Where do you feel stretched thin? Be honest and listen to what they have to say. Communication is everything!

5. Make a shared Google calendar. Name it "Power Couple" or something of the sort. Now you can see when the other is busy and plan your date nights with ease.

Wedding Bell Dolls

You will need: Music, a white pullout candle, sage, honey, dried rose petals, love incense, a small plate or coaster, newspaper, candle-carving supplies, love oil, glitter, hair from you and your partner

The best time to cast the spell: The full moon before your wedding

> 66 *Let's get traditional, bitches and witches! All kidding aside, congrats on finding someone worth marrying. That is a massive achievement. Let's perform a loving and protective candle spell to ensure that the wedding goes well and bless your sacred union. We are using white candles not because they represent purity, but because it's a protective color.*

Sex Witch says

The Spell:

1. Put on music that reminds you of your partner.

2. Take your white candle. If it's a pullout, remove it from the jar. Sage it inside and out.

3. Pour honey, to help you stick together and sweeten your love, into the bottom of the glass. Sprinkle dried rose petals on top.

4. Take a love incense, or a scent that reminds you of your partner, and hold the incense inside the glass so it fills up with smoke. Place a coaster or small plate on top of it.

5. Meanwhile, over newspaper, carve your name, your zodiac symbol, your partner's name, and their zodiac symbol into the candle.

6. Roll the candle in love oil until it's wet and sticky.

7. On the newspaper, sprinkle your glitter. You can't go wrong with pink or red, but for a more detailed look into color magick, visit the list on pages 3 and 4.

8. If you're that creep, sprinkle the snippets of your and your lover's hair on top of the glitter.

9. Roll the candle back and forth over the newspaper until it's covered in glitter.

10. Remove the plate or coaster on top of the glass and watch the smoke billow out. With a plunk, drop the candle back inside its glass casing.

11. It is now ready to burn! Place it on your love altar and light that wick. When the candle is finished burning, the spell is complete. And congrats finding someone worth marrying.

7. Magick for Protection

Witches need protection. This news may come as a surprise to city witches in liberal bubbles, but witches face persecution across the country. Have you ever read what an Evangelical website says about witchcraft? It's some hateful-ass shit. When you're independent, powerful, and go after what you want, the weak and the sheep will try to bring you down. That's not just for being a witch, that's just for having a sex drive—and especially if you date cis men. Tinder dates can become an actual life-or-death situation. This chapter on magick for protection contains basic uncrossing rituals all witches should know, as well as protection made explicitly for love and sex, such as rituals to remove clingy exes and how to protect secrets shared during a relationship. Use modern relationship advice paired with ancient occult tools to keep yourself safe on dating apps and on top of your sexual health.

Basic Uncrossing Candle

You will need: A white candle, sage, pen and paper, candle-carving tools, clearance or protection incense, uncrossing oil, newspaper, blue glitter

The best time to cast the spell: The waning moon

> 66 *People love to talk shit. People love to think shit! It's easy to feel worried and paranoid and trapped in a loop of wondering what fresh hell is happening next.*

Sex Witch says

Clear your mind and the negative influences of haters with this uncrossing candle. Perform this spell regularly when it's time to wipe away the cobwebs.

The Spell:

1. Set your supplies in front of you. Sage the white candle and yourself. Don't forget the bottoms of your feet! What do you wish to protect? Visualize yourself—perhaps yourself embracing your partner—surrounded by a shimmery white and blue orb that protects you from all negative influences.

2. Create a sigil. An easy and effective one for this spell is made using the word "PROTECTION." Draw a circle for O and cross out all the Os. Use your nice big O, and our sigil-making instructions, to create a protection sigil unique to your needs. While you draw the sigil, continue to visualize what you wish to protect.

3. Carve the sigil into the white candle. Add your name and the name of your partner. It's helpful to keep a mantra in your head while you work, such as "Sophie and Chad are protected from harm; their love is blessed by the sacred and profane."

4. Once you're finished carving, light your incense and let it billow over your candle.

5. Anoint the candle with a protection or uncrossing oil.

6. On newspaper to keep your floor from getting dirty, sprinkle blue glitter. Blue is the color of tranquility, peace, and protection. Roll the candle in the glitter.

7. Set it on your altar and light it. When the candle is finished burning, the spell is complete.

Get Over Former Lovers

You will need: Rose petals, coconut oil, a mortar and pestle, dragon's blood, Banishing Oil, salt, hair of a former partner, sage, a black human figure candle

The best time to cast the spell: The waning moon

> ❝❝ *Sometimes things don't work out. If everything did, life would be a lot less interesting. Still, that doesn't mean that breakups don't hurt. They can be more painful than death. Perhaps to protect ourselves from reality, we often view our former lovers through rose-colored glasses that prevent us from seeing the truth of the situation: that everything is as it should be, even when it hurts. This spell will kindly help you look at the situation clearly and get over your former lover (such a more glamorous term than ex).*

Sex Witch says

The Spell:

1. Take three red rose petals: one to represent you, one to represent your ex, and one to represent the relationship including the breakup. Soothe each petal by gently rubbing coconut oil onto the flower. Place the petals into your mortar and pestle.

2. Add three pieces of dragon's blood to strengthen the spell and aid in protection from hurt.

3. Pour in some Banishing Oil—enough to help mush the ingredients into a paste—and a sprinkle of salt to remove both rosy glasses and pain.

4. If you have hair saved of your former lover—which is a delightfully creepy next-level witch move—add that. Mash up the mixture using your mortar and pestle.

5. Sage your black candle to remove any energies picked up. Select whichever body for your candle that best represents your former lover. Somewhere safe to make a mess, anoint the candle with your magickal paste.

6. As you anoint the candle, say: "[Former lover's name], wherever you are, I now see things for how they are. Hurt and pain, burn away, make room for the glory of another day."

7. Place the candle somewhere safe and light it. Once it is finished burning, the spell is complete.

Protect Your Friendship with Benefits

You will need: Pink roses, water, honey, a mortar and pestle, pen and a paper, envelope

The best time to cast the spell: The full moon

Sex Witch says

    A friends with benefits situation can either be the best thing that happens to you or the worst. On a good day, you have incredible sex with someone you respect and care for as a friend in between breakups as your reliable sex go-to. On a bad day, someone falls in love—but not both of you—and the situation blows up leaving you friendless and sexless. Let's prevent that from happening by figuring out what you want and then protecting it.

The Spell:

1. Soak ten pink rose petals in four tablespoons of water for three hours. Mash the petals, rose water, and two tablespoons of honey using your mortar and pestle. Let the pink rose paste sit (this also doubles as a face mask, FYI).

2. Sit down, breathe deeply, and meditate to enter a calm mindset. Break out a pen and paper. Journal your feelings

regarding your friends with benefits situation. If you don't know where to start, just begin writing. This could be a description of the current situation: "Jon and I have been fucking on and off since college, and the dick is great, but . . ." or something of the sort. Eventually, the truth will come out. Is this just a friend with great dick? Or do you want them to be your boyfriend? Cough it out.

3. Once you're being honest with yourself, write a letter of protection. This could be a letter to protect your friendship from the chaos that comes with dating and sex or to protect your heart if feelings are involved. Fold it three ways and place it in an envelope. Seal the envelope. Take a dollop of your pink rose paste and press it down on the fold with your finger.

4. Place the envelope somewhere to dry, and then on your bookshelf, under the bed, or wherever your secret stash location is. Act upon the realizations about the relationship. Make sure your actions mirror the truth in your protective letter.

Exes Be Gone

You will need: A simple black candle

The best time to cast the spell: The waning moon

> ❝ It's hard being so desired. Magickal cocks and pussies are addictive, and coupled with your amazing personality and hilarious sense of humor, it's no wonder some exes have trouble moving on. Poor things, but they really ought to leave you alone, so you can freely go on to the next one. A black candle, chant, and the power of your will shall banish exes who do not respect your decision to end a relationship and continue to meddle in your love life.

Sex
Witch
says

The Spell:

1. Take care of practical matters first. Are you on good terms with your ex? Write them a succinct text or email letting them know that you wish them the best and perhaps friendship is in the cards someday, but right now you are ready to move on and need them to leave you alone. If they are hostile or do not respect your wishes, block them. Defriend them. Unfollow them. Do everything you can on your end to sever the connection.

2. We don't always need an elaborate ritual for candle spells. You have spent enough time on this person already. All you need is a simple black candle. It will absorb negative energy and then burn it away. Hold your black candle and think about all your anger, your fears, your sorrows, your frustrations, your compassion, and any and all emotions this ex brings up for you. Remember to breathe deeply.

3. Burn the candle. When it's finished, the spell is complete. Resist your own temptation to reach out to them. It will pass.

A Protection Prayer for Sex Workers

You will need: Your altar, an image of Saint Martha, a ritual goblet, red wine, flowers

The best time to cast this spell: We always need this spell.

Sex
Witch
says

Sex workers are holy and should be respected as such. Society loves sex workers: it's the oldest occupation for a reason, however never out loud. They're the butt of jokes. They're constantly fighting against repressive legislation. They're at a much higher risk for rape and violence yet are not offered protection. Still they make the

world go round. They make people happy. They're heal-
ers. Invoke Saint Martha the Dominator, represented by
the snake, to offer protection to sex workers. Yes, Saint
Martha is from the Bible. She is very down with witches,
though, and especially sex workers.

The Spell:

1. Not every spell must happen in one moment and involve setting something on fire. Sometimes we have long-term plans. Create this altar to Saint Martha for you, someone you know, or sex workers' rights.

2. First place a photo of Saint Martha on your altar. She is frequently portrayed with a serpent.

3. Keep the altar tidy and bring her lots of gifts. She likes the color red, wine, and flowers. Fill your goblet with wine and place it on the altar for Saint Martha or offer her flowers. There's no need to stick to a rigid schedule; honor her as you please.

4. Say the following prayer as an offering and protection spell: "Saint Martha the Dominator, protector of those who serve, give protection to all sex workers and bathe those who seek to silence such strong beings with love to heal their hate."

5. Don't be a SWERF (sex worker-exclusionary radical feminist, a woman who supports mainstream feminism but opposes sex work). Include sex workers in all feminist action.

Freeze Enemies

You will need: An image of your enemy or a piece of paper and pen, a freezer-safe container (ice cube trays work), water, a freezer

The best time to cast the spell: The waning moon

Sex Witch says

> *It might be an ex who won't stop bugging you to get back together. Perhaps some asshole is blowing up your phone trying to make you feel badly about a new relationship. No matter who or what it is, someone is interfering in your life, and it's annoying as hell. Let's put a stop to it. This freezing spell won't hurt anyone, it will simply prevent them from causing you harm.*

The Spell:

1. Obtain a photo of your enemy. You can print out a photo of them from social media. If a photo is unattainable, write their name on a piece of paper.

2. Fold up the photo or paper so it can fit into the container or ice cube tray you are using to freeze them.

3. Fill it up with water. As you do, whisper into the water: "I freeze you from causing me further harm."

4. Place them in your freezer. Keep them there as long as you want. One day you may be unconcerned with them and ready to toss them out. You may freeze as many enemies as you like!

Detect Lies

You will need: Tarot cards

The best time to cast the spell: Ideally this meditation is performed daily, first thing in the morning.

46 *The only truly effective form of lie detection is healthy communication. However, witches can boost their psychic power through daily meditation, intuition, the tarot, and healthy communication.*

The Spell:

1. Each morning, after you have your coffee and feel like a human being, grab your deck of tarot cards and sit down somewhere quiet. Close your eyes and meditate for a few minutes while holding your tarot deck.

2. When you're ready, with your eyes still closed begin shuffling the tarot deck. Ask the cards, "What do I need to know today?"

3. Stop shuffling and pull a card. Stare into it and let meaning arise. Remember that there is no tarot card to fear, not even the scary ones. The tarot in its entirety paints a portrait of the human experience. Each card is a slide of a life lesson we all experience at some point or another.

4. Place the deck with the card you drew facing up on your altar. Leave it there all day long. Throughout the day, notice how it pops up. Place the card back in the deck at the end of the day after reflecting on how it presented in your life.

5. Performing this meditation daily will strongly increase your psychic skills and intuition in addition to teaching you the tarot. Use these skills to pick up on gut feelings when someone is being dishonest with you while grounding yourself to prevent paranoia.

6. Tells of liars include giving vague, avoidant answers and grooming. However, the science on signs of lying is spotty. A much more effective way to get the truth out of someone is communication. Tell your partner: "You know, you can

always be honest with me. I'd always prefer the truth. We can talk and work through anything that arises like grown-ups. Our communication is very important to me as I want this relationship to work."

7. If someone is acting suspicious, pull a card to glean insight into what's going on and then talk to them about it. If they refuse to communicate or be honest with you, trust the sharp witch intuition and dump the asshole.

An Amulet for Legal Action

You will need: A tarot deck, a white candle, sage, candle-carving tools, and a necklace or charm of importance to you

Sex Witch says

66 *The last thing a witch wants is to come home to a subpoena. Talk about muggle problems! But it happens. So does divorce. Or we decide to report our rapist or fight back on a wrongful termination. We can't completely untangle ourselves from the legal system, but with this ritual, we can work our witchy ways to seek justice and protection.*

The best time to cast the spell: Whenever the authorities get involved

The Spell:

1. Call a lawyer. If you don't have or can't afford a lawyer, look into low-cost legal services in your area. A simple Google search should bring up results near you. Get your muggle plans in place before you move on to the magick.

2. Give yourself some time and space. Anything involving lawyers, police, and judges is capital S stressful. Acknowledge your trauma. Eat some cake, have some good sex, take a bath.

Engage in all your favorite forms of self-care to fill up your inner love tank.

3. Using your favorite tarot deck, take out the Justice card. In the Rider-Waite deck, Justice is depicted as an androgynous figure holding a sword and scales. Justice corresponds with Libra. It represents fairness, balance, and the workings of karma. Invoking Justice is a hex-free way to regain your power when someone has wronged you. Hold the card and meditate upon your situation and desired outcome.

4. Sage your white candle. Carve your name, zodiac symbol, and an image of the scales into it. Place it on your altar and light the fucker. Set the Justice card to its right.

5. During such stressful times, it is reassuring to wear an amulet of protection over your heart chakra. An amulet can be anything that makes you feel safe. It can be your grandmother's jewelry or a necklace you bought while traveling that brings up happy memories. In front of your altar, meditate holding your chosen amulet. Invoke the feeling of safety and confidence it inspires. Visualize your desired outcome. Keep the amulet on you during the legal proceedings until you feel called to take it off.

6. Keep reaching out to friends, family, and coven members for support. Snuggle extra with your familiars. You are not alone and will reach the other side. You're a goddamn witch after all.

Sexual Health Protection

You will need: Latex barriers such as condoms and dental dams, echinacea tincture, garlic tincture, lemon balm tincture, ginseng extract tincture, sambucus elderberry syrup, sage extract

The best time to cast the spell: During your slutty phase

Sex Witch says

> 66 *Use this herbal blend to boost immunity during peri-ods when you find yourself kissing many toads. This herbal blend in conjunction with safer sex practices such as latex barriers and regular STI screening will keep you on the right track.*

The Spell:

1. Congrats on being slutty and single! Enjoy every second of it. While there is no shame in STIs, and all of them, even HIV, are manageable today, most of us don't go collecting viruses. Your first step? Go get tested: know your status. Take care of what you need to take care of and stock up on free condoms and dental dams.

2. Hold potential lovers to the same standard that you hold yourself. Say, "Hey, I just got tested—what about you?"

3. Always use latex barriers and continue getting tested regularly, roughly every six months if you're living your full slut truth. If you come down with something or fear that you have, go to your doctor or local clinic.

4. Today being a witch means utilizing both the modern and wisewoman tools at our disposal. There is evidence to suggest that echinacea, garlic, sambucus (elderberry), ginseng, lemon balm, and sage all contain antiviral and immune-boosting properties. Mix the four tinctures, which are alcohol-based, and drop one vial under your tongue before a date. Brush your teeth to remove garlic breath.

5. Keep the sambucus syrup, which is delicious and healing, around and take a tablespoon whenever you please.

6. Remember that sage is not just for cleansing your home! While capsules and dried herbs are better than nothing, most herbalists agree that tinctures are the best method of effective delivery. Dose yourself with some antiviral sage the next time you sage your home to keep both of you clean.

Bury Secrets

You will need: A pen and paper, a mason jar, palo santo, honey, somewhere to bury the jar

The best time to cast the spell: The waning moon

> *After sex or over dinner—perhaps after a bottle of wine—we end up sharing secrets with our romantic partners. It's an exchange of intimacy that brings us closer to our partners and a bold and applaudable move. However, sometimes anxiety kicks in. Does he need to know about that time I tried to commit myself to a mental institution? We're not together anymore, but she still knows what I've done wasted inside of a taxi. Whatever your intimate information is, it can become worrisome after a breakup. Literally bury your secrets with a memento to signify the end of the relationship for peace of mind.*

Sex Witch says

The Spell:

1. Write down all the secrets you shared on a piece of paper. Rip them out one by one, fold them up, and place them in your jar.

2. Once the jar is filled, light the palo santo. The cleansing smoke of this holy wood is not only used to purify and remove your fear around such secrets, but acts as a confidence booster. The sacred smell can help calm you and remind you that even your darkest secrets are nothing to be ashamed of. Hold the lit palo santo in the jar and fill it up.

3. Warm up some honey and drizzle it into the jar. In this case, the honey is used to sweeten your secrets and comfort you. Even if your ex told every secret of yours to the world, you would be okay. You've already survived the worst part.

4. At night when no one can see you, bury your jar. If you don't have access to dirty locales, you can also drop it into a body of water. Your secrets are safe with nature, and you are free.

Act on Red Flags

You will need: A journal and pen

The best time to cast the spell: Ongoing

Sex Witch says

❝ Red flags are warning signs that someone may not be a good fit for us as a romantic partner. These are easy to ignore, though, especially while we are high on a new relationship. Keep a journal of your dating patterns and partners and follow this meditation to get brutally honest with yourself. Call in strength from your guides and act on red flags rather than ignoring them until they fester.

The Spell:

1. Sit cross-legged and begin deep breathing. Continue until a calm meditative state arises. Acknowledge all thoughts like falling leaves.

2. Write down your new lover's red flags in the journal. It may be their ex, their political views, a history of cheating, or unresolved trauma.

3. You don't have to end things, but you do have to be aware of what you're getting into. How does acknowledging their red flags make you feel? If you want to go running, ask yourself if you can live with that feeling. You don't have to act now. Say a prayer to your guides to ask for wisdom and intuitive help on knowing what is right. Or you might look at the list and scrawl "I fucking love you" underneath it because you know it doesn't matter. Trust yourself, witch.

Notes: Be aware of red flags. Write them down. If you're happy it doesn't have to end. There are always exceptions and opposites attract (no abuse). Call on your dating guides to protect you.

Erect Boundaries

You will need: Salt, a journal, a pen

The best time to cast the spell: When you're feeling overwhelmed and trying to balance work, friendship, and romance

> ❝ *Boundaries can save a romance. They should not be walls keeping your partner out, but are tools to keep you, the rest of your life, and your sanity intact.*

Sex Witch says

The Spell:

1. Sprinkle salt clockwise in a circle on the ground large enough for you to sit in. As you do, think of your relationship. Say, "These boundaries only serve to protect my relationship with [insert name of your lover]."

2. Sit inside the salt circle with your journal and pen. Close your eyes and visualize yourself as a whole independent being. In relationships it's easy to merge with the other person and lose our identity. We want to preserve ourselves and the other areas of our life so that we can stand tall next to our partner like two trees.

3. What else exists within your precious circle? Perhaps social media stalking gets you down and you want to stop that. Your friendships are crucial as they provide a support system separate from your partner, preventing you from relying on them entirely. Do you need alone time to recharge? Jot down everything you wish to protect as you enter into a union with another person.

4. When you're finished, open your eyes. Remember: Having boundaries and a separate life from your partner strengthens a relationship. Return to your salt circle whenever you need to recharge your independence.

Stay Safe on Dating Apps

You will need: Your phone, a pouch, condoms, lube packets, a phone charger, makeup-removing wipes, and pepper spray or another small weapon that won't get you arrested

The best time to cast the spell: Create this on-the-go kit when you match with someone you want to meet in real life and maybe even make out with.

Sex Witch says

    Dating apps are a good thing. You can meet and fuck fascinating and sexy people who you may have never connected with otherwise. However, there are also scammers and murderers. Use these tools and tips to stay safe while swiping.

The Spell:

1. Make the background of your phone an image evocative of what you wish to attract. Perhaps it is an image of the Lovers tarot card, or David Bowie, or red roses.

2. Start swiping. Don't be afraid to message first.

3. Put together a little pouch or slut bag. There is magick in the mundane. Keep condoms, lube, a phone charger, and makeup-removing wipes if you need them in your bag to have with you for any potential sleepovers.

4. Add a pepper spray or another safety precaution that you can't harm yourself with to fight off monsters should the worst come true.

5. There is nothing morally wrong with fucking on the first date. However, more than one date helps you sniff someone out. Consider waiting a few dates to go home with someone desirable out of precautions, not purity.

6. If the best comes true and you meet someone, don't freak out that it happened on a dating app. Enjoy it.

Become a Light Shield

You will need: Yourself

The best time to cast the spell: Whenever you need to feel confident and safe

> ❝ Witches are often taught to emanate a protective shield of light. This is helpful, but the advanced technique involves using your powers of visualization to turn your magickal body into an impermeable light shield.

Sex Witch says

The Spell:

1. Sit on the ground cross-legged somewhere safe and serene. Take a few moments to just sit in silence, breathing naturally, to relax and enter a meditative state.

2. Visualize a ball of light in your chest. It might be silver, perhaps a shimmery purple, or a bright gold. It may change colors. Whatever arises for you is right.

3. Continue to breathe and visualize that ball of protective light expanding throughout your chest. Slowly notice it spread throughout your torso and limbs and explode out through your toes and head until you are completely permeated with protective light.

4. Your inner light can form a bubble or protective shield but remember that it comes from within you. You have the power to protect yourself from psychic vampires or those that wish to take advantage of your emotional labor and leave you feeling drained all on your own.

Disarm Psychic Vampires

You will need: Yourself

The best time to cast the spell: When a vampiric asshole crosses your path

Sex Witch says

" *You may have heard about the evil eye, but did you know you can use your own stare and energy? Psychic vampires are people who only want to use you and drain you of your energy. They may remind you where the expression "toxic" comes from. Witches are stronger than vampires. Disarm them using an incantation and your stare.*

The Spell:

1. Turn yourself into a light shield. Become impermeable.

2. Learn to sense psychic vampires. They could be someone at a party, on the subway, a colleague, or even a romantic partner. They are someone insecure and weak who feeds off of your power and life force rather than curate their own. They may be fake nice or cruel and even abusive. Psychic vampires leave you feeling used up and drained.

3. If this person is someone you are close or intimate with, you'll need more than a stare. Please refer to the cord-cutting ritual on page 88. To shoo them away with a stare, step into the most confident version of yourself. You are not a human but a god. You have nothing to fear yet everyone fears you. You are filled to the brink with potent and protective magickal energy.

4. Direct that energy out through your eyes with the most viciously epic stare you can do. Look them straight in the eyes. Disarm them. This is beyond bitch face; we're giving out witch face.

5. If they are being verbally annoying, simply say, "Would you kindly stop talking?" "You're being inappropriate," or the more advanced, "Fuck off."

6. Walk away from the vampire with your energy intact.

8. Magick for Revenge

The desire for revenge or justice is an animal instinct experienced by all humans, just like sex. Rather than pretend like such thoughts don't arise in dating, this section faces the matter directly. As Bri Luna of The Hoodwitch taught me, if you can't hex, you can't heal. This is not a book for playing nice; this is a book about love—a human experience frequently likened to war. While hexes on homophobes, rapists, and racists are on the table without shame, when it comes to personal attacks, such as on exes or an ex's new partner, living well is the best revenge. We will not be doling out attacks on individuals who upset us, but rather obtaining revenge through our own health and success. These spells should be used only after becoming well-versed in protective magick.

Make Them Think of You

You will need: Your sexy-ass self, a mirror, sage, black tourmaline

The best time to cast the spell: At night when your target is asleep

> ❝ *Mirror, mirror, on the wall, who's the sexiest witch of all? You, obviously, but did your lover forget? Muggles can be such idiots. Mirrors appear in lore and fairy tales because they can act as a portal. While the mirror over the bed is a trope, it's bad feng shui to have a mirror*

Sex Witch says

facing your bed. This puts you at risk for unwanted spirits entering your home and psychic attacks! But in this spell, you are the unwanted spirit. Muah ha ha.

The Spell:

1. Invoke your inner Scorpio and act like a creep. Figure out your crush, lover, or former lover's bedtime.

2. Get naked, or put on your favorite party dress. Go natural, or do your makeup. Dress however you want to look when they think of you.

3. Sage your home and place black tourmaline near you for your own protection.

4. Sit in front of a mirror. Close your eyes. Practice deep breathing until you enter a trancelike state. Visualize your target asleep in their bed. Picture their face, what they're wearing, and their sleepy little head. People are more vulnerable to spellwork while they're sleeping.

5. Open your eyes. Stare into the mirror. Visualize yourself teleporting through the mirror into their bed. Enter their dreams. Become their obsession. Whisper in the ear. Tell them what you want them to know.

6. Come back to your home. Take a few more breaths. Undress or get dressed depending on how you decided to confront them, turn your mirror around, get some sleep, or go about your night.

Hex Homophobes

You will need: Newspaper, a black candle, rainbow glitter, candle-carving tools, a very gay playlist, sage, love oil or lube

The best time to cast the spell: The waning moon

66 *Sometimes witches need to fight back. Homophobic people use their hate, religious dogma, and often secret shame to hurt those whose love does not meet the strict definition of what's okay. Burn a black candle covered in rainbow glitter to throw them off their hateful agenda and fill the world with love for all.*

Sex Witch says

The Spell:

1. Set up your area. Glitter gets everywhere, but that can be an interior decorating style choice. Lay out newspaper on the floor. Place your black candle, rainbow glitter, and carving tools around the area.

2. Turn on your very gay playlist. What makes you LGBTQIA+ or ally proud? Britney? Bowie? Crank it up and dance. The queer version of meditation is dancing.

3. Light your sage, and dance around saging your home, as well as candle supplies, to smoke away any negative vibes or hate.

4. Sit down in front of your candle station. Pick up the black candle. Say the incantation: "Love wins, love is gay, hate is pathetic, I banish you away." Repeat until you feel fantastic.

5. Use your candle-carving tools to carve a rainbow into the black candle. Add the name and zodiac signs of you or any LGBTQIA+ folks you'd like to particularly protect.

6. Anoint the candle in a love oil or a lube—whatever works best between you and your god. Note: Lube is holy. It makes anal sex comfortable as well as vaginal sex. Keep it around and not just for spellwork.

7. Sprinkle rainbow glitter on your newspaper. Place your sticky candle in the middle. Pick up each side of the newspaper and roll the black candle until it's covered in rainbow glitter, representing the spectrum of sexuality.

8. Light the candle and let the hate burn away.

Get Rich

You will need: A spell bag, Money-Drawing Oil or coconut oil, a five-dollar bill, citrine

The best time to cast the spell: During the waxing moon

Sex Witch says

> **❝** *Beyoncé says the best revenge is your paper. Build your bank account with enough money to live the life of your dreams and forget about those who wronged you in your past. Attract money with this spell bag anointed in Money-Drawing Oil and filled with magickal objects that bring in cash. Wear the bag around your neck until it falls off; then your spell is complete.*

The Spell:

1. Meditate through several cycles of breaths. As you do, visualize your bank account on your computer screen. The number is obscenely high. But you're not ashamed. You earned and deserved every cent of that money. Would you prefer some rich white dude had it?

2. Take out your spell bag. Any small cloth bag, either worn around your neck or able to fit in your purse or pocket will do.

3. Optional: Put on Rihanna's "Bitch Better Have My Money."

4. Grab either Money-Drawing Oil, which can be purchased at occult stores and online, or coconut oil, which Venus, the

goddess of abundance, adores. Using your finger, lightly rub some oil inside the bag to anoint it with your intention.

5. Roll up the five-dollar bill like you're about to snort a line. Place the lucky fiver in your magick pouch.

6. Add a chunk of citrine, which is a crystal known for attracting career and money success.

7. Tie up the bag and place it around your neck, in your pocket, or in your purse. This spell is a long burn and that's okay. One day, the bag will fall apart, the contents will spill out, and the spell will be complete.

Find a Hot Rebound (Catch a Dick Potion)

You will need: Coconut oil, a small bottle or vial, dried rose petals, your period blood, vaginal fluid, or semen

The best time to cast the spell: Whenever you're horny, baby

> " *After a long relationship ends, it's healthy to enjoy consensual casual encounters before entering another commitment. Plus, hot sex can help us get over someone. Ensure that your hot rebound leads to orgasms rather than tears for your ex by making this secret recipe lust potion. Apply it behind your ears and around your genitals to attract the hot rebound—and hot rebound sex—of your dreams.*

Sex Witch says

The Spell:

1. Coconut oil is used to attract money, sex, and love and can be used as lube if you're in a fluid-bonded relationship and not using condoms. It also smells delicious. Use it as your base oil. Pour it three-quarters full in your bottle.

2. Buy yourself a red rose. Before it begins to rot, hang it upside down. This is the best method of drying roses. After about a week it will be fully dry. Take one petal and crumble it up into teeny rose bits. Sprinkle them carefully into your bottle.

3. Don't feel gross. Don't feel evil. Simply skip this step if it makes you uncomfortable. Collect some of your period blood, semen, or vaginal fluid. You just need enough to coat your finger and gently stick into your potion. Now it is ignited with your essence.

4. Before you go out on a date or dancing with friends, dab some on your neck and around your genitals. Get ready to drive everyone at the club wild with your scent.

Silence Slut-Shamers

You will need: A photo of your slut-shaming enemy, a black or metallic Sharpie, a mason jar, red glitter, dried rose petals, red wine

The best time to cast the spell: The waning moon

Sex Witch says

    ❝ *Slut-shaming is a form of sexual harassment. It is hate. It is the duty of witches to shut this up. But we won't bow down to a slut-shamer's level. We silence those jealous of our sexual freedom with love.*

The Spell:

1. Print out a photo of the person who is slut-shaming you. Get your Sharpie ready. State: "Your fear breeds hate, but love is great, silent you will stay" three times.

2. Scribble all over and across their mouth. Make a mess.

3. Fold up the photo and place it into the mason jar.

4. Sprinkle red glitter and dried rose petals on top. Pour red wine over them so they get a taste of their own medicine. (Magick loves puns.)

5. Screw it up tight and bury it. If you can't bury it, leave it at a crossroads.

A Tarot Spread to Reveal Secrets

You will need: A tarot deck

The best time to cast the spell: When your spidey senses are tingling that something is up

> *After a meditation for psychic strength, use a tarot spread to reveal the truth behind a situation that is alerting your witch instincts that something is amiss.*

Sex Witch says

The Spell:

1. Sit in front of your altar. Light candles. Place your tarot deck to your right.

2. Close your eyes. Breathe naturally for as long as you like. Trust yourself on this one. The more you meditate, the more you will sharpen your psychic abilities. If your intuition is telling you that something is wrong—listen to it. Do you suspect someone is cheating? Is the relationship just not right? Did they vote against their own best interests? Sit in a meditative state with the prompt "I know." You already know the answer. Tap into it.

3. When you're ready, spread your tarot cards in a half-moon in front of you. Hover your hand over the rainbow and pull three cards that speak to you.

4. Sometimes three-card spreads represent the past, the present, and the future. Don't stick to hard categories for this ritual, though. It's about intuition rather than a recipe. Use the cards as a tool of reflection rather than divination. You already know what's going on. Stare at the cards until they reflect it back at you.

5. As useful as tarot and meditation can be, we must still apply our witch tools in conjunction with the real world. Employ this ritual as a confidence boost to ask the person in question what's up. Don't accuse. Don't tell them what cards you pulled. Ideally in person, say: "Things feel off. It's unhealthy for me to try to guess. What's going on?" Even with all the spellwork in the world, a healthy relationship is impossible without communication.

Dump Them

You will need: Your friends

The best time to cast the spell: Ideally before you're bent over in a panic attack

Sex Witch says

66 *A beginner witch buys a cart of supplies and sets up an elaborate seven-day ritual when they want to leave a relationship. An advanced witch simple dumps them. This spell gives you the courage to just drop the motherfucker.*

The Spell:

1. Gather your coven. Let your most trusted friends know that you're about to dump your current lover. If it's a relationship you bitch about constantly, they will likely be very supportive and relieved. Ask your friends to make time for you in the days that follow the breakup. This way they are

prepared for your sobbing calls and power slut texts. And, in rare instances, if the shithead won't get off your couch, they can come and help remove him.

2. Book yourself a beauty appointment. What makes you feel hot? What can you afford? From haircuts to manicures, line up some vanity and self-care.

3. Get your adrenaline pumping to up your confidence. Go to the gym or dance until you sweat. We often stay in relationships because we're scared no one else will love us. You will be fighting off new advances within three months. You're a witch. Be with someone who makes you happy.

4. Break up with the shit. Be honest. If they're a shit, let them know that based on their behavior you can do better and are terminating the relationship. It's an announcement, not a discussion. If this is a sweet queer breakup, ask for space before revisiting friendship.

5. That's the spell, witch. Re-download Tinder.

Flourish in Flame

You will need: A piece of paper, a pen, cauldron, loose clearance incense, a lighter

The best time to cast the spell: The new moon

> 66 Build a fire in your cauldron to invoke your strength and vitality while burning away remnants of past relationships holding you back.

The Spell:

1. Write down all your emotions about your most recent breakup. Don't limit your words to your most recent ex if

Sex Witch says

you have built up hurt and trauma. Get all of that out of your head and onto a piece of paper.

2. Rip this list up into tiny pieces. Place the pieces in your cauldron.

3. You may want to cast this spell near a sink, or keep water or a fire extinguisher nearby, to practice fire safety and keep your worries down.

4. Sprinkle the loose clearance incense on top of the scraps in your cauldron. Light it all on fire.

5. Watch your worries and past hurts burn away, opening the door for fresh healing and new love.

Hex Your Rapist

You will need: A piece of paper, pen, mason jar, nails, cat shit and litter (if you have feline familiars), cayenne pepper, vinegar (or your own piss)

The best time to cast the spell: Whenever the fuck you want, survivor

> *Rape justifies a full-on hex. Put your rapist into a jar filled with vinegar and other ingredients and toss them into a body of water to ensure that what goes around comes around.*

The Spell:

1. Take care of your nonmagickal self first: Get a therapist who has experience working with survivors, make sure your family and close friends know what's happening, and work with your therapist and loved ones to ensure you have all the care you need. You deserve nothing less.

2. Write your rapist's name on a piece of paper. You can also print out their picture, but understandably, not everyone wants to look at their rapist. Do what feels right.

3. Crumple up that little shit's name or photo and stuff it in the jar. Don't be pretty about it. Toss nails in the jar. Put cat shit and litter in there—or your own shit or anything disgusting. This is your hex, witch.

4. Toss on cayenne pepper, which is used in spells to banish people.

5. Fill it up to the top with vinegar. Or, you can piss in it.

6. Screw the lid on tight. Toss the jar into a body of water. If a body of water is unavailable, leaving it at a crossroads works.

Balance Karma

You will need: Sage, candle-carving tools, a black pullout candle, red wine, iron fillings, dragon's blood incense, a coaster or something to stick on top of the candle jar, salt

The best time to cast the spell: The full moon

> *Create a karma-balancing candle to speed the usual process. This spell is extremely useful as it does not curate harm on others; it just asks karma to hurry up a little. Beware when practicing it that you too are beholden to the workings of the universe and your karma will catch up to you as well.*

Sex Witch says

The Spell:

1. Sage your magickal tools, the black candle, its glass case, and yourself.

2. Take a sip of red wine. Then pour a splash in the bottom of the glass candle jar.

3. Add a sprinkle of iron fillings at the base of the candle.

4. Light the dragon's blood incense and allow it to fill the base of the candle. Place a coaster on top to contain the smoke.

5. Using your candle-carving tools, carve a symbol of the scales into your black candle. For inspiration, look at artists' renditions online of Libra, which is the sign of justice, balance, and relationships.

6. Carve the name of the person you are seeking justice from and their zodiac sign into the candle as well.

7. Pour a few drops of red wine on your hand and use it to rub into the candle.

8. Remove the coaster and place the candle into its smoky jar.

9. Place the candle on your altar. Sprinkle a circle of salt around the candle to contain its energy.

10. Light the candle. When it is finished burning the spell is complete.

Put Your Partner's Pesky Exes in Their Place

You will need: Nine fruits, a bag

The best time to cast the spell: The waning moon

Sex Witch says

> *Sometimes it's not our partner or even our ex who is bothering us. Sometimes their exes or friends seem insistent on ensuring our life is hell. Absorb the adverse effects such people have on us with fruit, and then leave*

the fruit at the gates of a cemetery to put to rest their influence on us.

The Spell:

1. Is your partner's ex, like, haunting you? Do they pop into your brain at all times? Even worse—are they causing trouble between you and your partner? Sorry, bitch, they're mine now. Get this annoying-ass ex to leave you alone and put them where they belong: in a goddamn cemetery.

2. Strip naked. Think of your partner's ex. Think of all their meddling and annoying behavior. Get mad! Let your blood boil with all the reasons that you hate them. Scream if you want. Don't hold back.

3. Take your nine fruits and rub them over your body one by one. They are not just fruits from the grocery store: they are magickal sponges here to soak up all that toxicity. As you rub a fruit over your body, let it soak up all the hate you feel for this person. Let it absorb any power they have over you or within your relationship. Place the used fruit to the side in a bag.

4. Get dressed and go place the fruits at the cemetery gates. Leave them there. Do not look back once you walk away.

5. When you get home, take a shower to wash off any remaining energetic residue and to relax.

9. Magick for Healing

Witches are masters of transformation. We are healers not only for others, but of ourselves. While our hearts break like anyone else's, we have the tools to rise from the ashes stronger than before. Use this section to survive breakups and heal within to nurture the most important relationship: the one with yourself.

Boldness During a Breakup

You will need: A computer, makeup (including red lipstick), a mirror

The best time to cast the spell: Before going out partying

> This simple spell combines mirror and glamour magick coupled with the power of music to raise self-esteem and confidence levels while going through a breakup.

The Spell:

1. Make a playlist of all your favorite songs, but no sad songs allowed. There is a time for sobbing over losers and there is a time for feeling beautiful and glamorous: this is the latter. Name the playlist "I'm too good for you."

2. With your playlist blasting, do your makeup and hair in a style that makes you feel inhumanely hot. You are inhumanely

hot: after all, you're a witch! Curse that muggle for making you feel anything less than your fabulous self.

3. When you're ready, use red lipstick to write "HOT BITCH" on the mirror. Go forth, prosper, party, and get some. If your new lover sees your message . . . good!

Relationship Mending

You will need: A Sharpie, red felt, scissors, a needle and thread, coconut oil, dried rose petals, rosemary, a chunk of ginger, a bay leaf, a piece of your hair, a piece of your lover's hair

The best time to cast the spell: The waxing moon

Sex Witch says

> " *Literally stitch together a relationship using cloth and magickal herbs. This spell is for a relationship that went through a rough patch: the love is still there, but it merely needs a little healing.*

The Spell:

1. Using your Sharpie, draw a heart on your red felt. Bigger is better as it lends room for error. Cut it out. Now, trace your heart over the red felt to make a second heart. Cut that out as well.

2. On the inside of one heart, write your name. On the inside of the other, write your partner's name.

3. Using your needle and thread, begin sewing the bottom of the hearts together. It's okay if you have no idea how to sew. This is just for you.

4. Once you establish a base connection, rub some healing coconut oil inside the heart.

5. Sprinkle in dried rose petals. (The best way to dry rose petals is to hang a rose upside down using a hanger and leave for a week.)

6. Add a dash of rosemary. Rosemary is healing for all forms of love. While rose petals address romantic love, the rosemary helps repair the friendship in your relationship as well.

7. Add a chunk of fresh ginger for a dash of spice and excitement.

8. Add one bay leaf to bring the two of you together and ensure a lucky future.

9. Sew the hearts up almost the rest of the way.

10. Add a bit of your hair and some of your partner's. It's easy to get your partner's hair out of the shower or by creeping around in their home. Yes, you're a total creep, but DNA enhances a spell. Use the hair!

11. Sew the heart up all the way. Set it on your altar for seven days. During that time, do be an angel toward your partner. It's easy to turn into a bitch out of laziness in long-term relationships. Take one week off to be sweet and see how in conjunction with the spell your relationship mends.

Connect with Friends

You will need: Yellow flowers, newspaper, candle-carving tools, a yellow candle, your phone

The best time to cast the spell: Right now—you need human contact. Also, do this one during the day.

66 *Lean into your friendships for support and love rather than make your entire world about dating. This ritual uses yellow flowers and human contact to care for the platonic loves of our lives.*

The Spell:

1. Buy yourself yellow flowers such as yellow roses, carnations, marigolds, daisies, daffodils, or whatever you like, honey. Yellow signifies friendship and the sun, which represents life and abundance and joy—everything that friends can give you (and much more reliably than a romantic partner, at that). Place them in your home simply to brighten your mood. Can you think of a better reason?

2. Lay out your newspaper. Sit with your candle and candle-carving tools in sunlight. Carve a symbol of the sun into the candle. Add the names of your friends. Fit as many as you want on there. Add anyone who you're grateful for.

3. Place the candle on your altar and light it.

4. Call, text, or email every name you carved into that candle. Ask them how they are doing. Make plans for dinner. Put it in your calendar so you don't forget. Do not cancel plans. We cannot place the burden of being responsible for our joy all on our romantic partner. Maintaining friendships is crucial to the survival of your love life. We need people to bitch to and to be there for us should things fall apart.

Trust Issues: You Got 'Em

You will need: A journal and pen, a chunk of rose quartz

The best time to cast the spell: Whenever you're ready to acknowledge that your current partner isn't the reason that you're being a bitch to your current partner

> 66 *Practice this journaling ritual to identify and then address trust issues created from past trauma that get in the way of accepting deserved love into your life.*

The Spell:

1. How are your trust issues currently manifesting in your life? Grab your journal and pen and get ready to drag yourself. Write down everything that makes you feel distrustful. Your list may include: *They still love their ex. His mom hates me so he's obviously going to dump me. I'm too crazy. She's going to leave me.*

2. Examine what you wrote. Now write down the real reasons behind such trust concerns. Has your partner indicated that they still love their ex, or are you just insecure because they're richer than you? So his mom hates you. Is he a pussy like your ex who did what his parents wanted because they had money, or is he his own person?

3. Now create a third and final list of all the evidence your partner is trustworthy. Perhaps begin with: *They put up with my bullshit trust issues.*

4. Put your notebook down. Grab your rose quartz. Hold it to your heart. Close your eyes. Meditate on all the ways you are loved. Let the healing crystal soak up the nasty thoughts that say you're undeserving of love. Remember when Nick Cave told us to let love in?

5. Call up your partner and tell them how much you appreciate them.

Stop Contacting Your Ex

You will need: To face facts (and chocolate)

The best time to cast the spell: ASAP—you're embarrassing yourself.

Sex Witch says

66 *Breakups are severely traumatic. You lost someone. There is no overestimating the pain of what you're experiencing. But emailing, texting, or calling your ex is not the solution. Stop it. Seriously. Is there a chance of reconciliation? I don't know. But I do know that now is not the time. Everyone needs to heal. Heartbreak is not sexy. Here's how to stop contacting your ex.*

The Spell:

1. Delete their number from your phone. Write it down in the corner page of a book somewhere if you must, but delete it now. Unfollow them and unfriend them on all social media accounts. Better yet—delete and unfollow their friends and family, too.

2. Change your phone background to an image that gives you strength. This might be an animal, friends, yourself, or the Strength tarot card.

3. Eat some chocolate. Get those serotonin levels up.

Bed Cleansing Ritual

You will need: Palo santo, new sheets, pink roses, small spray bottle, water

The best time to cast the spell: Begin this spell during the waning moon phase and put on your new sheets on the first day of a new moon.

" *Get rid of those sheets covered in the DNA of your past partner! This ritual allows you to work within your budget to cleanse your bed of ex residue and create a love nest that incites excitement for the future and self-satisfaction.*

The Spell:

1. Light palo santo and wave the cleansing smoke throughout your bedroom, concentrating over the bed.

2. Buy new sheets. It's worth the cost. Follow your bedroom's current color scheme or select new ones based on color magick. For instance, blue brings tranquility and peace. Red promotes passion, and pink is a kinder self-love.

3. Make your own holy rose water. Pick up some pink roses. Pink represents love but is kind and gentle. Pink's mixture of sexy and sweet is the perfect potion to bless your new bedsheets. Pluck off six pink rose petals and place them in a small spray bottle. Fill it up with water. Before putting the top on, whisper "love, honor, respect, sex" into the water so it may carry these gifts, which you are wholly deserving of, into your bed.

4. On the first day of a new moon, a day of new beginnings, throw out your old sheets and put on the fresh ones.

5. Spritz the holy rose water on the sheets.

6. Climb into your bed and masturbate to consummate the space.

Queen Bitch Makeover

You will need: Magazines, glue, scissors, a notebook or poster, enough money to change your hair, your phone

The best time to cast the spell: Avoid changes to your appearance during Venus retrograde. Friday is the day of Venus, goddess of beauty, but we all work too hard to plan around the schedule of a goddess. Book your appointment whenever!

Sex Witch says

66 *It's not cliché to change your hair after a breakup; it's glamour magick. Express your freedom after a breakup using this glamour spell.*

The Spell:

1. If you went through a breakup, you deserve an ego boost. Lean into vanity and start thinking about updating your look. Focus on changing your hair.

2. You could make a Pinterest board, or you could go old-school. Make an inspiration board of your look. Let's say you want an orange bob. Go through magazines and cut out the latest orange hair trends. Print out some David Bowie circa Ziggy Stardust photos. Remember Leeloo from the *5th Element*? Create a glamorous mood board. Your dream hairstyle will come to you.

3. Schedule your day to implement your new hairstyle. That can mean a ten-dollar bottle of Manic Panic or a full four-hundred-dollar double process, cut, and style. Do whatever you want that works with your budget. Go get it done. Woohoo!

4. Take so many selfies. Don't be embarrassed about having breakup hair. Lean into it. Use the hashtag #breakuphair or #newlysingle. I double dare you!

Protection Prayer for Sexual Assault Survivors

You will need: A statue or drawing of the dark mother goddess Kali, a red candle, wine or menstrual blood

The best time to cast the spell: When you wish to send a survivor strength

> 66 *Invoke the demon-slaying power of mother goddess Kali to honor all sexual assault survivors and protect them from the cruelness of society as they live day to day with bravery.*

Sex Witch says

The Spell:

1. Obtain a statue or drawing of Kali. The Hindi goddess is the dark mother. She slays demons. She gets angry. She kills. She protects. She consumes what she desires. She is holy. She is loving. She is fierce. She is a complicated goddess who understands the complexities of sexual assault in ways mainstream American society does not. Place an image of her in your home for protection and strength.

2. Kali enjoys a blood offering. Anoint your red candle in either menstrual blood or red wine.

3. Light the candle. As you watch it burn bright red, say the name of survivors you wish to protect. This can be you, a friend, or a celebrity. State, "Thank you, [name of person], for your strength, I honor you! Kali Ma loves and protects us all." Repeat for as many names as you wish.

So Someone Cheated

You will need: Sage, passionflower tea, four white candles, a tarot deck, a journal and pen, a friend (optional)

The best time to cast the spell: Cheating can cause heartache beyond imagining. Cast this spell whenever you need it.

❝ *Cheating can feel like a literal stab to the heart. In addition to pain, cheating also brings up confusion. Why did they cheat? Is the relationship over? Are they truly sorry? Was it just sex or is there romance at stake? How you decide to handle cheating is up to you. There is no wrong or right answer. This spell simply helps provide clarity. While it can be done alone, if you have a friend you trust and need some company for this one please invite them over.*

The Spell:

1. Sage your entire home. That cheater was in here, likely lying and crying. Let's get rid of that nasty energy.

2. Brew a cup of passionflower tea. It's an herb associated with love that also has profound relaxing effects. Sip on it throughout the ritual to invoke and ingest love and calm.

3. Place a white candle at each corner of your bed. Purify your sacred sex space.

4. Shuffle your tarot deck while sitting in bed. When they feel ready, spread out the cards in front of you in a half-moon shape.

5. Let's get some insight. Keep your journal and pen nearby for notes. Ask the cards why they cheated. Intuitively pull three cards relating to their affair: One for the past, one for the present, and one for the future. Gaze at the cards and reflect on their desires and motivations. People cheat for a plethora of reasons. There is no handbook for this, only you and your intuition.

6. Now pull another three cards, past, present, and future, for your relationship. Sit with them for as long as you like.

7. Write down any thoughts, insights, questions, or revelations. The tarot is sacred, but it is a better mirror than mind reader. Ask your partner the same questions you asked the tarot. Take your time. Be honest. Require that your partner is equally honest. You know in your heart what the right move is. Trust that it will come to you and remember how strong you are.

Cut Cords

You will need: Black cotton rope, a black candle, a goblet, pomegranate juice, a ritual dagger

The best time to cast the spell: The new moon

> ❝ You know after a breakup, when it doesn't matter how long it's been, you just can't get that fucker out of your head? It's like they crawled inside of you and you think of them even though you don't want to. You want to be over them, but you're still connected somehow. Cord cutting is a ritual to help you sever ties. Don't worry: if a repaired future of friendship is in the cards, you can still do this spell. It's not a permanent banishing ritual. Think of it as trimming unhealthy split ends.

Sex Witch says

The Spell:

1. Sit down with the black cord, the candle, and a goblet full of pomegranate juice.

2. Light the black candle and place it directly in front of you.

3. Wrap the cord loosely around each wrist with plenty of slack in the middle. You don't have to be a shibari expert or a sailor.

4. Close your eyes. Visualize a cord coming out of your chest and connecting to the object of your ritual. See them. Stare

at the one who has been haunting you. Send them love even if you hate them. Repeat: "I am free, Raise my sword, Heal with love, Cut the cord."

5. Using all the emotional strength you have, visualize a giant cosmic sword slicing through the rotting cord connecting you to your ex-partner.

6. Open your eyes. Now use your dominant hand and slice through the literal black cord binding you with your ritual dagger. Toss the remains to the side.

7. Drink a goblet of pomegranate juice. In addition to its antioxidant properties, lore states that Persephone ate pomegranate to stay in the underworld with Hades, not as an act of control but because it gave her knowledge. She liked the underworld. You are in control of where, what, and who you connect yourself to.

Cleanse and Come

You will need: A vacuum and other muggle cleaning supplies, a broom (witchy and muggley!), palo santo, bath salts, a water-proof vibrator (optional)

The best time to cast the spell: Perform this cleansing ritual as soon as you break up with someone, especially if they lived with you and spent a lot of time in your home.

Sex Witch says

    Practice this ritual after you've finally gotten someone out of your life who caused pain. Cleanse your home both magickally and traditionally to get rid of energetic and physical debris. Celebrate the new sacred space by performing sex magick in the bath.

The Spell:

1. Get out your cleaning supplies. That motherfucker left their skin cells and Satan knows what else all over. Wash your sheets, vacuum and mop the floors, bleach the toilet, clean until your home sparkles. Throw out any of your ex's items left behind.

2. Light palo santo. Like sage, the sacred wood palo santo cleanses spaces energetically. While sage is said to remove all energies, palo santo is said to only remove negative energies while bringing in positive ones. You need some love after that shithead.

3. Once you're done physically cleaning, take a bath. Pour the bath salts into the running water to help your body relax and detoxify.

4. Get in. Bring your vibrator if you'd like. Masturbate. As you do, visualize what the next stage of your life will be like. Do you have more time for your career now? Are you ready to slut it up? Do you want alone time? To meet someone better suited for you? Let's do some sex magick. As you come in your bathtub, turning the water holy with your orgasm, visualize the life you're stepping into.

5. Get out of the bath. When you let the water out, all the negativity from your past relationship will swirl away down the drain. Now go enjoy your clean apartment.

Purify Your Pussy; Sage Your Cock

You will need: Sage

The best time to cast the spell: The new moon

> *They say that you can't unsuck a cock, but such a statement is obviously intended for muggles. Use this quick ritual to sage your genitals and all fuck holes as you would your home after a breakup.*

The Spell:

1. Get totally naked.

2. Light sage. Sage your pussy, your cock, your ass, your mouth, and anywhere that has ex energy clinging to it. Do not hold the burning sage directly on your skin but fan the smoke lightly around the area.

3. Bye-bye! Time to meet some new DNA.

Bathe in Enemy's Blood

You will need: Black latex or nitrile gloves, mortar and pestle, dragon's blood, baking soda, citric acid, Epsom salts, cornstarch, coconut oil, red food dye, mixing bowls, measuring cups and spoons, a whisk, bath bomb mold (a muffin tin works too), cannabis (optional but fun)

The best time to cast the spell: When you have a few hours to kill and don't mind getting messy

> *Fuck the haters. I don't care if it's your ex, someone at work, or your partner's judgmental mother. They do not deserve to distract you from your best life. Follow this ritual to ceremoniously bathe in their blood and exert your power over them by letting that shit go.*

The Spell:

1. First, we must make our bath bombs. Put on your black disposable gloves—we're going to get messy. Of course, any gloves would work, but black gloves look dominant and sexy.

2. Get out your mortar and pestle and dragon's blood. Dragon's blood is naturally red plant resin. It's used to increase the potency in spells. Take two or three chunks and grind them into powder.

3. Combine the 1 cup baking soda, ½ cup citric acid, ½ cup Epsom salts, ½ cup cornstarch, and your ground dragon's blood in a mixing bowl.

4. In a separate bowl, combine 2 tablespoons of warm/room temperature coconut oil (you just don't want it to be solid), 1 teaspoon water, 10 drops of red food dye. (The dragon's blood will make your mixture red on its own. If you prefer your bath bomb all natural, stick with dragon's blood. However, if you don't care about dyes and want your bath to be as bloody as possible, go for the added dye.)

5. Slowly drizzle the wet mixture into the dry while continuously whisking. The consistency should be like crumbly sand—not too wet, or the bomb will start going off before you're ready for it!

6. Tightly pack the mixture into a bath bomb mold. You want it tighter than virgin pussy. Let it form overnight.

7. Gently crack it open the next day. Tap around the edges using a spoon if it doesn't want to come out and play.

8. Now for the bath! If you partake in cannabis, please get high to expand your mind as much as possible.

9. Draw a bath. Make it hot. Drop the bath bomb into the tub and watch it go off, swirling and whirling around the water turning it bright red with the blood of your enemies. Lie back. You did avenge yourself. You won. You're bathing in their fucking blood. Do you have to pee? Pee in the bath to further dominate your dead enemies.

10. Once you feel relaxed enough to no longer give a shit about your enemies, get out of the tub and drain the water. A light bleach spray will remove the red residue.

A Ritual to Recover from Gaslighting

You will need: Your favorite costume, clothing, makeup, whatever makes you feel confident, a pillow (optional), a mirror

The best time to cast the spell: Whenever you need an ego boost

Sex Witch says

> 66 *Gaslighting is a technique in which the abuser makes you doubt the validity of your own thoughts. They may tell you that you're crazy, twist the truth about the past, and use other manipulation tactics to try and dominate you or kill rational thoughts. The goal is to control you by making you feel small. If you've been through it, you need self-love and to get that self-esteem back to where it should be.*

The Spell:

1. I'm sorry that someone gaslit you. It is horrifying, painful, and damaging to question your own thoughts and sanity. Give yourself a hug for getting out of the situation.

2. Get dressed up. Do your makeup. Yes, you can go out and party later! Or you can solo Netflix and chill. The goal is to feel sexy AF.

3. Let's remove some of that anger first. Scream "FUCK YOU" at the top of your lungs. Worried about the neighbors hearing? Scream into a pillow.

4. If you really filled up that pillow with rage, throw it out. If that's not budget-friendly, at least wash the case.

5. Now look in the mirror. See how beautiful you are! You're an angel from heaven that we do not deserve. Stare into your own gorgeous eyes and say the incantation: "I'm right." Repeat over and over as needed.

6. If your abuser ever reaches out, feel free to block them or reply: "FUCK YOU" and then block them.

7. Use "I'm right" like it's your fucking mantra. Get a tattoo.

Remove Cynicism

You will need: Devil card from the tarot, newspaper, a seven-day white pullout candle, clearance incense, a ritual dagger, clearance oil

The best time to cast the spell: The waning moon

> " *The world breaks our heart into a million pieces. Are you even living an interesting life if you don't have emotional scar tissue? Trust no one—but don't let such a revelation keep you from love and pleasure. Cast this spell to use your life experience as knowledge that doesn't get in the way of enjoying good sex and love.*

Sex Witch says

The Spell:

1. Pull out the Devil card from your tarot deck. In the Rider-Waite deck, the devil sits before a man and woman in chains. Upon closer inspection, though, you notice that the shackles are loose enough to step out of. They remain in bondage by their own choice. Is this card just a kink scene? Perhaps. It reminds us that even when we sit with the devil, the chains are always optional. How can you use your own chains for knowledge? Lucifer is the enlightened one, after all.

2. Spread out newspaper because candle carving is messy! Remove the white candle from its jar. Light clearance incense and watch it pour over the white candle.

3. Take your ritual dagger and carve an image of a sword into the candle. Swords represent intellect and are used to slice through the rope that binds us.

4. Carve your name and zodiac symbol just to make sure the gods know it's you.

5. Pour clearance oil into your hands and massage it all over the candle.

6. Light the thing. As it burns, what's jaded and holding you back burns away, leaving behind only knowledge.

Forgive Yourself

You will need: Wine, tea, or cannabis, a journal and pen, white candles, bath salts, white flowers

The best time to cast the spell: The waning moon

Sex Witch says

       We all fuck up. We cheat. We lie. We take out our own issues on others. We drink too much and say the wrong thing. Shit happens. It's important to own up to our mistakes, but after an apology it's time to learn from them and forgive ourselves. This can be the hardest part. Use this spell to let go of shame and forgive yourself to move on with life.

The Spell:

1. Sip some wine, puff some weed, or have a cup of tea. Do what you gotta do to relax. Then begin writing in your

journal. Write about what you did, how it hurt you and your relationship, and how the pain remains.

2. Light white candles around your bathroom. White signifies purification. Turn off harsh overhead lights.

3. Draw yourself a bath. Pour salts, which purify, into the bathwater. Lower yourself into the bath. Let the salts relax your muscles and draw out tension and stress.

4. When you're ready, get out of the bath and towel dry yourself. Then, while you're still naked, brush your body with the white flowers. Let the pretty petals brush off guilt and shame.

5. Go back to your journal. Write the words "I forgive myself" over and over until your hand hurts.

6. Make a list of what you learned from your mistake and how you will do better.

7. Bury the white flowers and your journal entries in soil. A backyard works, or if you live in a concrete jungle, you can leave them at a crossroads.

Conclusion

Here's what I know: due to trauma, insecurities, and centuries of negative programming, most of us are a bit messed up when it comes to love and sex. Sex positivity, promoting the freedom to be our most natural selves, is something we should all work toward. And witchcraft is a tool to help us get there.

Witchcraft mirrors life. The new moon, barely observable to the eye, grows larger until it's at its magnificent full form again. A full moon, ripe for manifestation, wanes away until the night is dark as black. So, too, do our desires and relationships wax and wane.

Spellcasting can help you identify what you desire and then go after it. So, what do you want? Marriage? A casual Tuesday night gangbang? Figuring out what you want is the first step in getting what you want out of love. A coven can be a mysterious secret society or just a group of friends hanging out. Community can help you make smart decisions in dating. Find yours.

This spellbook contains magickal instructions; rituals that have been handed down over centuries. But the one ingredient, the most important ingredient in any spell, is you. You must realize how powerful you are. You have to be a little selfish to do this. That doesn't mean you have to be an asshole. You have to learn to identify, advocate for, and then go after your needs from a place of confidence. Nothing is sexier than confidence. When you're sure of yourself, you can ask what you want in bed. You can ask for the money you deserve at work. And when evil strikes, you're not afraid to show some teeth.

Witchcraft is all about realizing and embracing your power. I hope this book has helped you find yours.

Resource List

I have compiled a list of resources to support you as you travel further down your magickal path. These are books that helped me realize and embrace my power. Some are iconic magickal texts, and others are the most modern take on the subject, such as astrology written by my most trusted magickal confidants. I have also included some websites where you can learn more about witchcraft, purchase ethically sourced magickal tools, and learn about your sexuality. Being a Sex Witch is all about realizing and embracing your power. I hope these sources help you find yours.

Recommended Reading

The Astrology of Love & Sex by Annabel Gat (Chronicle Books, 2019).

Becoming Dangerous: Witchy Femmes, Queer Conjurers, and Magical Rebels on Summoning the Power to Resist edited by Katie West and Jasmine Elliott (Fiction & Feeling, 2018).

The Book of Lies by Aleister Crowley (Weiser Books, 1981).

The Book of the Law by Aleister Crowley (Weiser Books, 1938).

The Crystal Bible: A Definitive Guide to Crystals by Judy Hall (Walking Stick Press, 2003).

The Enchanted Candle: Casting and Crafting Magickal Light by Lady Rhea (Magickal Realms Inc., 1986).

Inner Witch: A Modern Guide to the Ancient Craft by
Gabriela Herstik (Penguin Random House, 2018).

Light Magic for Dark Times: More than 100 Spells, Rituals, and Practices for Coping in a Crisis by Lisa Marie
Basile (Quarto Publishing Group, 2018).

Love Magic: A Handbook of Spells, Charms, and Potions by
Melissa West (Wellfleet Press, 2018).

*The Modern Witchcraft Book of Love Spells: Your Complete
Guide to Attracting Passion, Love, and Romance* by
Skye Alexander (Adams Media, 2017).

Revolutionary Witchcraft: A Guide to Magical Activism by
Sarah Lyons (Hachette Book Group Inc., 2019).

The Satanic Bible by Anton Szandor LaVey (Avon Books,
1969).

The Satanic Witch by Anton Szandor LaVey (Feral House,
1970).

Witches, Sluts, Feminists: Conjuring the Sex Positive by
Kristen J. Sollée (ThreeL Media, 2017).

*Women Who Run With the Wolves: Myths and Stories of
the Wild Woman Archetype* by Clarissa Pinkola Estés
(Random House, 1992).

Helpful Websites

www.babeland.com

Babeland sells LGBTQIA+-friendly, high-quality, and body-safe sex toys and wellness products.

www.fetlife.com

FetLife is a social network for kinky people. You can use it to browse, explore, and get to know your own sexual interests or meet other like-minded folks.

www.thehoodwitch.com

The Hoodwitch offers insightful articles about witchcraft as well as an online store that contains unique tarot decks and ethically sourced crystals.

www.originalbotanica.com

Original Botanica is a Bronx-based real-life botanica that sells many of the tools mentioned in this book such as pullout candles, potions, oils, and incenses.

www.mountainroseherbs.com

Mountain Rose Herbs sells a wide variety of high-quality sustainably sourced herbs. I love making infusions with their nettle leaves!

www.witchbabysoap.com

Witch Baby Soap makes the most beautiful, fun, and effective skin care, beauty, and bath products out there. The company is owned by a real-life and amazing witch, who is obviously a Taurus given her dedication to the luxury of decadent beauty (did I mention coffin-shaped bath bombs?).

About the Author

Sophie Saint Thomas is an acclaimed, queer, sex writer and witch living in New York and originally from the Virgin Islands. She has been a columnist for *VICE*, a producer at MTV Networks, and is currently a full-time freelance writer. She has contributed to *GQ*, *Allure*, *Glamour*, *VICE*, *Marie Claire*, *PRIDE*, *Cosmopolitan*, *Harper's Bazaar*, *Playboy*, *Noisey*, *Broadly*, *High Times*, *Refinery29*, *Mic*, *Nylon*, and *Gawker* (RIP) among others. She is the witchcraft columnist for "Queer Sex Coven" with *Autostraddle*. In July of 2019, Saint Thomas became the resident astrologer at *Allure*. She is the author of *Finding Your Higher Self* and *The Little Book of CBD for Self-Care*.

To Our Readers

Weiser Books, an imprint of Red Wheel/Weiser, publishes books across the entire spectrum of occult, esoteric, speculative, and New Age subjects. Our mission is to publish quality books that will make a difference in people's lives without advocating any one particular path or field of study. We value the integrity, originality, and depth of knowledge of our authors.

Our readers are our most important resource, and we appreciate your input, suggestions, and ideas about what you would like to see published.

Visit our website at *www.redwheelweiser.com* to learn about our upcoming books and free downloads, and be sure to go to *www.redwheelweiser.com/newsletter* to sign up for newsletters and exclusive offers.

You can also contact us at *info@rwwbooks.com* or at

Red Wheel/Weiser, LLC
65 Parker Street, Suite 7
Newburyport, MA 01950